BEEF HANOI SOUP • SPRING ROLLS • SHRIMP ON
SUGAR CANE • SAIGON SOUP • VIETNAMESE CURRY •
LAQUÉ DUCK WITH RICE NOODLES

This is just a sampling of 150 beguiling recipes, including classic and
modern dishes from the three gastronomic regions of Vietnam.

—Complete range of recipes from simple family dishes to elaborate
party fare.
—Special section on traditional Vietnamese favorites.
—Chapter on vegetarian and vegetable cooking, with detailed
instructions for making bean curd at home.
—Hints on advance preparation and easy-to-prepare dishes.
—Special sections on sauces, menu planning, and shopping sources.
—Clear instructions and careful attention to detail to assure perfect
results.
—Glossary with description of all necessary special ingredients,
their uses, and easily available substitutes.
—Lively and charming text, full of historical lore, anecdotes, and
notes on Vietnamese customs.

BACH NGÔ was born in Vietnam and studied at virtually all of Saigon's
cooking schools. She and her family came to the U.S. in 1975 after the fall
of Saigon. When the city was being evacuated, her husband gave her 30
minutes to pack up the household. Bach gathered up her children and her
priceless recipe files, leaving everything else behind. She now lives with her
family in Connecticut where she runs two branches of her Vietnamese
restaurant Chez Bach.

GLORIA ZIMMERMAN, an authority on Eastern cuisine, has conducted
her own Chinese cooking school and taught with the renowned Grace Chu.

THE CLASSIC CUISINE OF VIETNAM

BACH NGO & GLORIA ZIMMERMAN

A PLUME BOOK

To Ben and Nhon

PLUME
Published by the Penguin Group
Penguin Books USA Inc., 375 Hudson Street, New York, New York 10014,
U.S.A.
Penguin Books Ltd, 27 Wrights Lane, London W8 5TZ, England
Penguin Books Australia Ltd, Ringwood, Victoria, Australia
Penguin Books Canada Ltd, 2801 John Street, Markham, Ontario, Canada
L3R 1B4
Penguin Books (N.Z.) Ltd, 182-190 Wairau Road, Auckland 10, New Zealand

Penguin Books Ltd, Registered Offices: Harmondsworth, Middlesex, England

Published by Plume, an imprint of New American Library, a division of
Penguin Books USA Inc.

Published by arrangement with Barron's Educational Series, Inc.

The line drawings are by Milton Glaser, Inc.

 REGISTERED TRADEMARK—MARCA REGISTRADA

Library of Congress Cataloging-in-Publication Data

Bach, Ngô.
    The classic cuisine of Vietnam.

    Reprint. Originally published: New York: Barron's/Woodbury, © 1979.
    Includes index.
    1. Cookery, Vietnamese.   I. Zimmerman, Gloria.
II. Title.
[TX724.5.V5B32   1986]   641.59597   85-28332
ISBN 0-452-25833-2

First Plume Printing, April, 1986

    6   7   8   9   10   11   12   13   14

PRINTED IN THE UNITED STATES OF AMERICA

CONTENTS

Foreword by Jacques Pépin

Along with the explosion of cooking schools, gourmet shops, cookware stores, and restaurants throughout the country, there have been scores of cookbooks that have appeared in the last few years. Chinese, French, Japanese, Russian, Greek, and Italian cooking has been investigated as *haute cuisine* as well as family cooking and ethnic food. However, surprisingly enough, the cuisine of Vietnam has never been translated for the average cook into a readable or useful book.

Luckily for me I had been introduced to Vietnamese food as a child in France. A great number of Vietnamese restaurants compete with the best restaurants in Paris and the quality and identity of their cuisine has been sufficient to make them prosperous for years. The Vietnam conflict is probably the main reason why up until now, no serious attempts have been made to popularize such cooking in this country. However life goes on, and the cuisine of Vietnam, fortunately, has survived the war and has enough individuality to attract cooks all over the world.

To my knowledge, no book of much value has emerged in the United States in recent years, which is dedicated to the cuisine of Vietnam. Here now we have a good book on the subject.

Over 1,000 books appear each year and unfortunately, through this plethora of new books, there aren't that many worth reading or following. For a book to be good, it must be honest, knowledgeable, and written in such a way that it is readable and the recipes can be followed. Such is this book that Bạch Ngô and Gloria Zimmerman are introducing. Most new cookbooks are simply re-workings of old recipes, or sometimes actual old recipes are taken from several books and compiled into a "new" cookbook. *The Classic Cuisine of Vietnam* is good because it is honest, because both authors know their subject, and because the recipes are authentic and work. The ingredients are listed and explained, and sources of supply are given for exotic foods. Where an original ingredient may be unavailable, in the United States, a substitute is given, adapted by the authors, with ingredients readily available in this coun-

try. Some history is given in clear, concise terms at the beginning of the book, which helps in the comprehension of it as a whole. The recipes are simple, original, and delectable. I have tasted and tested several of these recipes and have had great feasts in my house with Vietnamese food.

The Classic Cuisine of Vietnam explains thoroughly what makes things work, and shows different techniques explained by the authors. I am sure that after you have tried some of them, you will be hooked as I am on Vietnamese cooking. Keep cooking and *bon appétit,* or *chúc ăn ngon,* as they say in Vietnamese!

Introduction

Anyone under the illusion that Vietnamese cookery is a mere variation of Chinese cuisine will discover what a fundamentally different style it has — and unforgettably different delight it is. A similar comparison could be made between French and Italian cuisine, each using many of the same raw materials with sharply varying techniques and, just as important, different flavorings and spices, with infinitely different results.

As the four-thousand-year-old Chinese culture produced a cuisine world renowned for its exquisite sophistication, Vietnamese culture, zealously guarded and nurtured over the same time span, has given birth to a cuisine no less sophisticated. Craig Claiborne, eminent food critic of the *New York Times,* hails the Vietnamese kitchen as "among the most outstanding on earth." In France, the temple of *haute cuisine,* Vietnamese restaurants now far outnumber Chinese, not only in Paris but throughout the rest of the country, and the tide of discovery has moved across the Atlantic. Food-conscious Americans, both young and old, are now joyously discovering Vietnam's delicate and beguiling food-making art.

What are the differences between these ancient cuisines, both rooted in cultures predating Western civilization by thousands of years?

The major differences lie in the seasonings employed, the techniques used, and the differing emphasis on basic ingredients.

Soy sauce, the universal Chinese seasoning, is rarely seen in Vietnamese recipes, which rely on *nước mắm* (pronounced *nyuk mahm*) instead. *Nước mắm* is the product of layers of fresh anchovies and layers of salt, laid down in large barrels. The process produces a clear amber liquid, a bit salty and redolent of the sea. The literal translation into English — "fish sauce" — does not come near to conveying its remarkable quality of blending. *Nước mắm* is used as a flavoring in the cooking process and as a base for Nước Chấm (page 34) — a combination of *nước mắm*, garlic, chili peppers, fresh lime, and sugar that accompanies almost all dishes and takes the place of salt at the table. Insidiously good, it has the unique property of submerging itself in the flavors of other ingredients, adding a strikingly delicious dimension to this exotic cookery.

Shallots, very infrequently seen in the Chinese kitchen, are used in great abundance by the Vietnamese. On the other hand, neither lamb nor mutton are to be found in Vietnam. However, fresh herbs and seasonings such as coriander and scallions are utilized plentifully. Lemon grass, or citronella root, unknown in Chinese cookery, accents many Vietnamese dishes with its lemon-scented flavor.

Stir-frying in oil is probably the most widely used technique in Chinese cookery. In the Vietnamese kitchen, however, the use of oil is minuscule, and when it appears is used in much smaller amounts; simmering is probably the single most widely used technique employed by the Vietnamese. Large quantities of cornstarch are frequently used by the Chinese, whereas the Vietnamese only occasionally use thickening agents, and in very small amounts.

Although they never appear in Chinese cuisine, fresh, uncooked vegetables and salads are an integral part of most Vietnamese meals. The fresh vegetable platter will always include lettuce, cucumbers, coriander, and mint, of which there are many varieties, and, among others not available here, sliced green bananas, *tía tô* (a leafy vegetable with a strong taste of mint), and *rau diếp cá*, which has a taste suggestive of the seashore.

Taken all in all, the deemphasis on fats and thickening agents as well as the large, fresh, uncooked vegetable component easily explain the lack of surfeit experienced after a hearty Vietnamese meal.

The characteristics of Vietnamese cuisine probably account for its remarkable growth in France, where the highly publicized *nouvelle cuisine* was recently "created" with much the same qualities. Although Vietnamese cuisine dates back thousands of years, it may well be dubbed "the *nouvelle cuisine* of Oriental cookery."

A genuine mystery, still unsolved, contradicts all the lessons of history. The Chinese military conquest of Vietnam and occupation for a thousand years, with repeated attempts at a reconquest, should have overwhelmed Vietnamese culture to the point of its disappearance — typically the fate of other conquered cultures. Despite historical precedent, the Vietnamese retained their own language, folk culture, and customs, and after throwing off the Chinese yoke, they emerged with a keenly developed sense of their complex, sophisticated — and separate — identity.

Although by American standards Vietnam is a small country (about the size of New Mexico), it stretches for over a thousand miles along the eastern coast of the Southeast Asian peninsula. The major centers of population are in the North and South, connected by a long narrow stretch of mountainous country referred to as "the Center." Both the North, with the Red River Delta, and the South, with its Mekong River Delta, are very fertile, low-lying country.

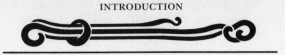

The regional cuisines are similarly divided: Hanoi in the North, Hue in the Center, and Saigon in the South. Although, as elsewhere, there are local dialects, the Vietnamese speak only one language. Although it has many Chinese loan words, the Vietnamese language is related to Chinese only to the same extent that English, containing many French loan words, is related to French.

The food of each region is a distinct reflection of all the richly varied forms that history and geography have stamped upon the cuisine of Vietnam.

So it is that the food of the North, in colder latitudes, with a smaller variety of ingredients and few spices available, is somewhat lighter and less spicily hot, with black pepper a widely used condiment. Curiously enough, although seafood such as crab is enormously popular, fish comprise a surprisingly minor part of northern menus. Stir-fried dishes appear more frequently in the North than in the Center or the South, no doubt due to the massive presence of China on its borders.

The cuisine of the Center, where Hué, the ancient capital of the kings of Vietnam, is located, reflects the pleasures of the royal palate in the highly decorative presentation of foods and in the meals, which tend to consist of small portions of many dishes. Foods are very spicy, as evidenced by the frequent use of hot chili peppers and shrimp sauce.

The South, with its hot, humid climate and fertile fields, has a great variety of vegetables, fruits, meat, and game. The influence of the French is more pronounced here, seen in the more frequent use of such vegetables as white potatoes and asparagus, among others. These were introduced by the French and are grown in the central highlands, with its temperate climate; they are all prepared, however, with the distinctive Vietnamese flair. Over the centuries Indian culture has had a definite impact, apparent in the popularity of curried dishes. Sugar and sugar cane, produced locally, are in more widespread use in the South than in the other regions.

France has its own regional kitchen, each proud of its specialties; yet the tradition of *haute cuisine* remains the hallmark of French gastronomy. So it is in Vietnam. Although each region does have its own style, the lines of distinction between them are blurred. Where ingredients for another regional specialty are not available, creative adaptions are developed. Dishes characteristic of the North are very popular in the South—Hanoi Soup (page 52) for example—and the reverse is true as well.

All the ingredients in our recipes are available in the West, either in supermarkets, Oriental groceries, or by mail order from the suppliers listed on pages 242–43. We have described equipment and techniques in detail; most of the techniques are familiar, and those that are unfamiliar are easily mastered, so *Chúc quí bạn thành công*— happy cooking!

Equipment

Outside of a mortar and pestle, Vietnamese cooking requires no equipment other than that found in most Western kitchens.

In Vietnam a wok, shallower than the Chinese wok, is used for stir-frying. Since she came to the United States, however, Bạch has been using frying pans, and she finds them quite adequate. In addition to larger pots and frying pans, there is a particular need for very small pans. When you prepare our recipes, you will realize that very small amounts of food are cooked, particularly meats and seafood, and you will be assured of a much better finished product if you use vessels of the right size. For example, if you are simmering half a pound of meat or fish, it is more logical to cook that amount in a small pot for better results and for more economy. Traditionally, every Vietnamese family owns an assortment of really tiny pots.

While some of the foods we use can be prepared in a blender or food processor, *nước chấm* — the very important sauce served at almost all meals — must be prepared with a mortar and pestle.

We have made a list to help you:

Frying pans, several sizes. This group should include a 7- or 8-inch nonstick frying pan for making rice papers, a heavy one with a cover, and a smaller one for toasting rice, seeds, peanuts, and so on. A wok would also be useful.

Saucepans in various sizes, including some very small ones, with covers, for simmering.

A large pot for boiling stock.

Also, and in more detail:

Blender

For pulverizing seeds, mixing batters, making coconut milk, and so forth.

Mortar and Pestle

For making *nước chấm* or for pounding meat or shrimp. For *nước chấm*, a normal-sized ceramic or stone mortar and pestle are required. For heavier work, like pounding meat or shrimp, a heavier, larger stone mortar and pestle are needed. However, in many recipes food processors can be very satisfactory work-saving substitutes, and where this is the case we have so indicated.

Food Processors

Optional. In Vietnam, the many pâtés are purchased ready made from special stores. Vietnamese abroad have now discovered that the pâtés they miss so much can be prepared with the food processor.

Knives

Preparation of food for any cuisine requires the use of several sharp knives of the best quality one can afford. Good equipment will last a lifetime with proper care. A good French chef's knife or a standard-weight number 3 Chinese cleaver are especially suitable for cutting meat and vegetables; they are not recommended for cutting through bones. We recommend a *heavy* number 3 Chinese cleaver for cutting through poultry and fish bones. Also of great convenience is a boning knife, for removing bones from chicken parts, whole poultry, or meat.

Many cooks recommend carbon-steel knives. While such knives do hold a sharp edge longer, they have the disadvantage of discoloring certain ingredients (e.g., onion) and rusting if not carefully dried. Stainless steel is very hard and almost impossible to sharpen. However, Henckels and some other knife makers produce a no-stain high-carbon-steel blade, including a Chinese-style cleaver, which eliminates the disadvantage of carbon steel. We recommend this type of knife.

Carrot Peeler

We are all familiar with the swivel-action peelers. In our recipes we use this peeler for cutting paper-thin slices of vegetables, usually carrots for Carrot Salad (page 38), and other recipes. In Vietnam, we have another peeler, very similar in design to the carrot peeler although a bit cruder in construction. It has a wider blade, which makes it possible to cut a much wider strip, and it is also made of a much heavier metal. We actually found one in a store in New York's Chinatown — it is excellent for peeling sugar cane, as well as cutting wider, paper-thin strips of vegetables.

Charcoal Stoves or Barbecues

We use this for all cooking in Vietnam—barbecuing, simmering, boiling. (See Barbecuing in the chapter on Techniques, pages 29–31.)

Steamer

An authentic Vietnamese steamer is made of metal, usually aluminum. It consists of a pot in which water is boiled and at least two more metal inserts (restaurant steamers usually have five) that fit directly on the lower pot of water, one above the other. These inserts are perforated, allowing wet steam to circulate freely through them, enabling either a large quantity of one food or several different foods to be cooked at the same time.

You can improvise a steamer by placing the bowl of food to be steamed in a large pot or roasting pan, making sure the sides of the bowl are high enough so the water comes halfway up. You can then cover the steamer and proceed with the recipe. If the bowl with the food is too shallow and you are afraid water is going to spill over into it, it would be best to place a rack with feet about 2 inches in height into the pan and then rest your dish on that.

Steamers and racks can be purchased in Oriental grocery stores.

Electric Rice Cooker

Although this is not an essential piece of equipment, most Oriental kitchens that boast electricity do have an electric rice cooker. It provides the cook with an extra burner, and there is no need to watch the pot. Simply put the right amount of rice and water into the cooker, press a button, and lo and behold — in half an hour the rice is ready, and perfect. Some rice cookers come with thermostats that will keep the rice hot for up to 5 hours.

Chopsticks

The Vietnamese cook uses a long pair of bamboo chopsticks for stirring and cooking, never the stirrer or spatula that the Chinese cook uses for stir-frying. Standard-size bamboo chopsticks are used for beating, turning, and mixing.

Ingredients

Although Vietnamese cuisine is, for Westerners, exotic, most of the ingredients — meats, seafood, vegetables, and even many of the flavorings — are familiar and readily available. Our list of ingredients consists essentially of those items important in the Vietnamese kitchen but not generally encountered by the reader. All these ingredients are available either at the supermarket or at Oriental grocers. Only one—*tương*—may require ordering by mail. In any case, the lists of sources of supply include mail-order houses. With each day that passes, all these ingredients are becoming increasingly obtainable, so the reader will find a quick perusal of the ingredients list quite reassuring.

Nevertheless, we have indicated substitutes for many ingredients. Only those substitutes that will work well in the recipes have been suggested, so as to maintain their inherent qualities.

We suggest the purchase of small quantities until you gradually familiarize yourself with the ingredients and develop your own list of staples for those recipes you most enjoy.

Agar-Agar

Made in different forms from various seaweeds, agar-agar serves as a gelatin. We will be using the form which we like best, in strands. Instructions for its use will be found with the recipe for Jellied Chicken (page 127). It needs no refrigeration and will keep indefinitely.

Alum

For keeping foods crunchy, an important characteristic in Vietnamese cooking. Used in fruit recipes, Pickled Pigs' Ears (page 90), and wherever that

crisp texture is wanted. Found in Oriental groceries, it resembles rock sugar except that it has a clearer color. Just break off as large a piece as you need.

Anchovy Sauce

In Vietnam, available already prepared. In the West, we have been able to find Philippine anchovy sauce, but it is not compatible with the Vietnamese taste. Until we are able to buy the Vietnamese anchovy sauce, Bạch has developed an excellent recipe for it, which we use in our Beef Fondue with Vinegar (pages 184–85).

Bamboo Shoots

Best fresh, although in the West fresh bamboo shoots are virtually unobtainable. However, all Oriental groceries carry canned bamboo shoots. If you are able to purchase fresh bamboo shoots, they must be peeled and boiled. The canned bamboo shoots need no further preparation. After opening the can, they will keep for up to 3 weeks in the refrigerator if covered with water that is changed every 2 days.

DRIED BAMBOO SHOOTS: These must be soaked and boiled. In the mountains of Vietnam there are huge bamboo forests, where bamboo shoots are cut and processed, then sent to market in very large pieces. In the West, when we can buy them, they are boxed and cut in small slices; we find the best brand to be Companion. They are not a substitute for fresh or canned bamboo shoots. They are specifically called for in certain recipes and have their own unique flavor and texture.

SOUR BAMBOO SHOOTS: These are used in the preparation of Sour Fish Head Soup (page 183). In the West we buy them in cans (Companion brand again the best). In Vietnam you either prepare sour bamboo at home or buy it fresh in the market.

Banana Leaves

These are used in Vietnamese cooking for wrapping various foods, particularly cakes and pâtés. The cakes are not sweet dessert cakes, as in Western

cooking, but a rather substantial food, such as glutinous rice, shaped into a cake. When wrapped in banana leaves, a delicate green hue is transferred to the rice. Here, however, aluminum foil makes a satisfactory substitute.

Bean Curd

Made from soybeans, bean curd is an important source of protein and is obtainable in all Oriental groceries. In appearance it resembles a soft white custard. Bean curd has no pronounced flavor of its own but absorbs the flavors of the foods with which it is cooked. There is no substitute, but we have an excellent recipe for making your own at home (see pages 158–59). After it is purchased or prepared, it should be submerged in water and refrigerated until needed. It is very perishable and keeps only about 5 days.

Bean Sprouts

These are the sprouts of mung beans, available in Oriental groceries, in many supermarkets, or you can easily grow your own (see page 160). They do come in cans but are limp and soggy, and we prefer to eliminate them from the recipe if we cannot get them fresh. When you buy them, rinse and put into a bowl of cold water, uncovered. Refrigerate and they will keep for about 5 days.

Bok Choy

Also known as "Chinese cabbage," this is a very mild vegetable, actually a member of the Swiss chard family. It has an elongated shape and very white stems with dark green leaves. Its construction is similar to that of celery.

Cellophane Noodles

See Noodles.

Chili Peppers

Red, fresh, or dried. We prefer the fresh, but in northern climates they are available only during the warmer seasons. They must be red. If these peppers are not allowed to ripen to the red stage and are still green, they will not be spicy hot, as they should be for our recipes. The red chili pepper will be found in almost all Center recipes.

Chinese Parsley

See Coriander.

Chinese Sausages

These are usually made by the Chinese people in Vietnam. In the United States, they are generally available in Chinese groceries. The best ones are imported from Canada. There is no substitute.

Coconut

Generally available. It should be heavy, and you should be able to hear the liquid sloshing around.

COCONUT WATER: From fresh green coconuts. We do not use the meat of these coconuts, just the clear water inside that is surrounded by the coconut meat.

COCONUT MILK: Made from the meat of the brown-shelled coconut. The coconut shell must be broken first. Instructions for opening the coconut and making coconut milk will be found under Basic Recipes on page 48. It is not easy to get a really fresh ripe coconut outside the tropical climate where it grows, so canned coconut milk is an excellent substitute for the fresh — and sometimes even better. Do not buy coconut cream; it is not a substitute for

coconut milk. We have found the best available brand of coconut milk is Stanfood. It is highly concentrated, and Bạch now prefers this to the fresh coconuts available outside her country. When a recipe calls for coconut milk, open the 12-ounce can it comes in and add enough water to make up the volume needed.

Coriander

Fresh coriander, also known as "Chinese parsley" and "cilantro," is available in Oriental groceries, Latin American groceries, and in some supermarkets. Widely used in Vietnamese cooking sprinkled on soups, served with spring rolls, and as a decorative garnish. It has a unique flavor and there is no substitute. Try growing it in your garden or even in a windowbox if not obtainable. It grows quickly and easily.

Cornstarch

Used as a thickener, and sometimes to coat ingredients before frying. In Vietnamese cooking we use very little thickening — much less than in Chinese.

Dried Shrimp

Generally used in small amounts in Oriental recipes, as they have a very strong flavor. Soak them in warm water before cooking. They can be stored in a jar without refrigeration.

Dried Squid

A fishy-smelling and -tasting version of fresh squid. Can be stored for long periods in the pantry. Available in Oriental grocery stores.

Fish Sauce (*nước mắm*)

Fish sauce is to Vietnamese cooking what salt is to Western and soy sauce to Chinese cooking. It is included in practically all recipes. Prepared from fresh anchovies and salt, layered in huge wooden barrels, the manufacture of fish sauce is a major industry. The factories are located along the coast to assure the freshness of the fish to be processed. Fermentation is started once a year, during the fishing season. After about 3 months in the barrel, liquid drips from an open spigot, to be poured back into the top of the barrel. After about 6 months the fish sauce is produced.

The first draining is the very best fish sauce, lighter in color and perfectly clear. It is relatively expensive and is reserved for table use. The second and third drainings yield a fish sauce of lower quality and lower cost for general-purpose cooking. The two towns most noted for their fish sauce are Phú Quốc and Phan Thiết. Phú Quốc produces the best fish sauce, some of which is exported. On the label, the word *nhi* signifies the highest quality. When fish sauce manufactured in Vietnam is not available, that of Thailand or Hong Kong is quite acceptable. Philippine or Chinese fish sauce will not be satisfactory. For table use and available in all Oriental groceries is Squid Brand Fish Sauce, the best one on the market. Whatever brand, look for *Cá Cơm* on the label, which means that only anchovies were used — an indication of the highest quality for table use.

Five Spice Powder

Used in Vietnamese cooking occasionally, five spice powder is a much more important flavoring in Chinese cooking. It is a combination of ground star anise, cinnamon, cloves, fennel, and Szechuan peppercorns. It can be stored in a dry place for about a year.

Garlic

Used universally in all cooking, garlic is an essential ingredient in Vietnamese cuisine. By gently tapping the garlic with the flat of a knife, you can easily remove the skin and then proceed with your recipe, always remembering to remove and discard the hard tip of the clove.

Gingerroot

Used only occasionally in Vietnamese cooking, gingerroot has a very special flavor, unlike any other, and is always used fresh. Dried ginger bears no resemblance to the fresh and should never be used as a substitute. Readily available in Oriental groceries and in many supermarkets, it does not last indefinitely and turns woody after a few weeks in the refrigerator. To store for a much longer period, peel and rinse in cold water and put it into a jar. Cover with pale dry sherry and refrigerate. Some people store it in their freezers, well wrapped, and cut off a piece as needed. However, the crispness is lost in the freezer.

Glutinous Rice

See Rice.

Jellyfish

Whole jellyfish are sold dried, in which form they can be stored on a shelf for an indefinite period. Before using, they must be soaked. Practically flavorless, but their crunchiness adds an interesting texture to the dishes in which they are used. Available in Oriental grocery stores.

Leeks

Always used in Buddhist dishes in place of garlic and scallions, as well as in some vegetable soups, leeks are available all year round. They resemble scallions in appearance but are much thicker and broader, and in flavor they are sweeter. The inside of the leek is very sandy, and you can either cut it vertically through the center and rinse it, or you can make several slashes through the white part without actually cutting the entire leek in half. Wash under running water. The French usually use the slash method of washing leeks, but in our recipes they are always cut before cooking.

Lemon Grass (Citronella root)

This is a tropical grass much used in Vietnamese cuisine. The lower part of the stem, up to where the leaves start branching out, is the edible portion. The loose leaves and upper two-thirds are discarded, and the lower part, resembling white of scallion, is either cut or chopped, according to the recipe. You can buy it readily in Paris, California, and all Vietnamese and some Chinese groceries. As a substitute we have used the dried variety (definitely not the powdered), which we soak for 2 hours in hot water and then chop very fine. It's quite good. If you live in a moderate climate, and if you manage to get fresh lemon grass, root and all, put it out in your garden and it will multiply rapidly. Otherwise you can grow it in the spring and summer. It keeps well indoors, in a flowerpot; in the refrigerator for a few months; and chopped and frozen for a year.

Lettuce

By this we mean Boston or leaf lettuce, used in the many vegetable platters or salads served at Vietnamese meals. We prefer a soft variety of lettuce, one that is easy to use as a wrapper in addition to its use as a salad.

Lily Buds or Flowers

These dried flowers have a very delicate flavor. They must be soaked for about 30 minutes before using, then rinsed until the water runs clear and the stem or hard tip removed. The recipe will always give instructions as to how they are to be used, cut crosswise or tied into a knot. They can be stored for years in a jar in a dry place.

Maggi Sauce

A good example of the French influence. Used by all Vietnamese as a condiment, and one of the first items a Vietnamese in a new country buys for his table. Used very sparingly (a few drops at most) and to taste.

Mint (*quế, rau thởm, tiá tô, húng*)

In Vietnam many varieties are used. In the West, however, we are more limited in the kinds of mint we are able to obtain. We have been using common mint and a small curly mint. In the colder climate we have been unable to get fresh mint in the wintertime, and we never use dried mint, so we simply omit it. Fresh mint is always part of the Vietnamese vegetable platter, which is present at almost every meal (see Basic Recipes, pages 37–38). It is usually rolled with other vegetables in Vietnamese spring rolls, in fresh and dried rice papers, and in numerous other dishes. We do grow it in our gardens in the summertime and on occasion have managed to purchase some at a local greenhouse when it's not in season.

Mung Beans

From green-skinned mung beans we grow the popular bean sprout. See Bean Sprouts (page 13) and page 160 for growing bean sprouts.

Yellow mung beans are mung beans dried and with the green skins removed. We use them similarly to the way people in the West use beans. They come packaged in 1-pound plastic bags and can be purchased in Oriental groceries.

Mushrooms, Dried

Chinese or Japanese dried mushrooms, which have a very special flavor. Although you can substitute fresh mushrooms, you will lose the flavor called for in a particular dish. Available in Oriental groceries and some specialty shops, they are unlike any European dried mushroom and are therefore not interchangeable. They must be soaked before use for at least 30 minutes, and the hard stem should be removed. They are fairly expensive and vary in quality from a very thin to a thicker, meatier cap, the thicker being better and, naturally, more expensive. You can buy as little as a 1-ounce package, as they are used quite sparingly. Store in a jar in a dry place.

Noodles

CELLOPHANE NOODLES: These dried noodles, made from mung beans, are also used a great deal in Chinese cooking. The Vietnamese prefer the more elastic cellophane noodles. You can ascertain which brand will be more elastic by comparing them. The noodles that are more translucent in the package will be more elastic after cooking than those that are very white in the package. They come in 2-, 4-, and 8-ounce packages and must be soaked before cooking. One of our favorite brands to date is labeled "Lungkow Vermicelli."

RICE STICKS (bánh phở): For Hanoi Soup (see page 52). Made from rice, the medium-size sticks are the correct size. They are ¼ inch wide and are made in Thailand. In Vietnam they are available fresh, but in the West we must make do with the dried variety, which can be found in Oriental groceries throughout the country. In California and France, because of the large influx of Vietnamese people, all Vietnamese ingredients, fresh as well as dried, are available.

RICE STICKS (bún): Foo Lung Ching Kee, Inc., Hong Kong — this particular brand of rice sticks cannot be distinguished from the fresh rice noodles of Vietnam. These dried noodles are stringlike in appearance and expand to double their size, becoming very white, when cooked. They are an ingredient in many soups and are also served with barbecued meats and fondues. Japanese alimentary paste noodles *somen* are a good substitute.

RICE VERMICELLI or RICE STICKS (bánh hỏi): Thinnest available, stringlike, as the *bún* above, but even thinner. Egret or Summit brands are readily available.

JAPANESE ALIMENTARY PASTE NOODLES (somen): Although they are made from wheat flour, these serve as a good substitute for the rice sticks (*bún*) above. They are packaged in 1-pound boxes, each containing 5 ribbon-tied individual packets of noodles. We find Summit brand very satisfactory.

Oil

For cooking, use any unflavored vegetable oil such as corn, peanut, or soy bean oil. For deep frying, peanut oil tends to keep the food crisper. For those

on a low-cholesterol diet, corn oil would be desirable. Until recently the Vietnamese used lard, which they themselves had rendered. However, with the advent of vegetable oils at a lower cost and greater convenience, neither lard nor any other solid shortening is in use.

SESAME OIL: Be sure to buy the Oriental sesame oil prepared from roasted sesame seeds. The variety sold in health food stores is prepared from raw sesame seeds and should not be used in our recipes.

Oyster Sauce

A thick brown sauce made of oysters and soy sauce. Available in bottles, it is excellent for flavoring chicken, beef, and seafood. Sold in Oriental grocery stores and can be stored on a shelf or for long periods in a refrigerator.

Papaya

A delicious tropical fruit, there are many varieties of papaya in Vietnam, some a foot in length. When green, it is used in cooking and for some very special salads. When the papaya turns yellow, it is eaten as a fruit.

Bạch's Great-Aunt Tân, one of the wives of Khải Định, a king of Vietnam and father of Bảo Đại, the last king, still lives in Vietnam. She has always had a very special talent for making beautiful papaya butterflies and flowers. When there is an important family party, Aunt Tân always appears with a bag full of these beautiful decorations.

Peanuts

We use raw peanuts, with red skins, and generally toast them before using (see Basic Recipes, page 46). Used in many recipes, cooked, and also in desserts and as a garnish, they are available in 1-pound packages in Oriental groceries. They keep well in a dry place.

Pepper

BLACK PEPPER: In Vietnam we use both black and white whole pepper-corns, which are ground fresh in a mill before each use. The people of the North use a great deal of black pepper, much more than the Center and the South.

PICKLED GREEN PEPPERCORNS: Frequently served as an accompaniment to alcoholic drinks. Tài Nam, a special restaurant in Saigon where these are served, is especially popular with the drinking crowd.

Pineapple, Fresh

Used in soups, fondues, and stir-fried dishes. We never use canned pineap-ple as a substitute.

Potato Starch

In Vietnamese cuisine, used as a binder for pâtés. Available in supermarkets under various brand names, and in Oriental groceries as *katakuri-ko*, Hime brand.

Preserved Vegetable (*tân xại*)

Even in Vietnam, this is regarded as a Chinese vegetable. Packed in a jar or a crock, it consists of tiny pieces of Chinese cabbage, marinated and then dried. Usually used to enhance the flavor of soups, it is available in all Oriental groceries.

Rice

SWEET OR GLUTINOUS RICE: A short-grain rice, quite sticky when cooked, used in special recipes and much more widely used in Vietnamese than in Chinese cooking.

EXTRA-LONG-GRAIN RICE: Available in supermarkets and Oriental groceries. A brand such as Carolina in the United States is excellent, but if one does a great deal of Vietnamese cooking, it is more economical to purchase a 25-pound bag of rice in an Oriental grocery. Always ask for long-grain rice.

Rice Flour

This is rice ground to a very fine powder. We have experimented with various brands and find the Chinese Tienley brand to be our favorite, although other brands are acceptable.

Rice Papers, Dried (*bánh tráng*)

There is no substitute for the Vietnamese rice paper. It is a round, tissue-thin, brittle crêpe, made of rice, salt, and water. After the rice papers are formed, they are placed on bamboo mats to dry out in the sun; hence the intricate crosshatch pattern embedded in each paper. Before use the rice paper must be dampened, and after a few seconds it becomes flexible and ready for filling.

Used for wrapping the famous *chả giò* (Vietnamese spring roll), rice papers are much crisper than any Chinese wrapper with which Westerners are familiar. Rice papers are also used to wrap foods that are eaten uncooked.

We have included a few recipes for this very important Vietnamese food. The manufacture of rice papers is a major industry in Vietnam, and they are becoming increasingly available in Oriental stores in the West, mostly imported from Thailand.

Roasted Rice Powder

A flavoring you can prepare. You will find it in Basic Recipes, page 47.

Rice Sticks

See Noodles.

Rock Sugar (rock candy)

Amber-colored, clear crystallized sugar. Used to flavor some dishes and to give a glaze to some sauces. This can be purchased by the pound in Oriental grocery stores as well as candy and gourmet shops. Store at room temperature in a covered container.

Scallions

Also known as "green onions," the scallion is closely related to the onion, but with a slender stalk of long green leaves and a white lower section. Used a great deal in Vietnamese cooking, both in cooked dishes and as a garnish, especially for the many soups. Often chopped together with coriander or alone. The white part is used as a substitute for shallots.

Sesame Oil

See Oil.

Sesame Seeds

These can be obtained in Oriental grocery stores in larger packages than those available in supermarkets. We usually toast them (see Basic Recipes, page 46) just before using or we use them raw in marinades. You will find recipes using sesame seeds in various ways throughout the book.

Shallots

Small, brown-skinned members of the onion family, shallots grow in clusters similar to garlic and taste slightly of garlic. A very important flavoring in Vietnamese cooking; a substitute is the white part of scallions (see above).

Shrimp Chips

A crisp cracker prepared from fresh shrimp, tapioca starch, and egg white. Vietnam's long seacoast yields an abundance of shrimp, much of which goes into the manufacture of shrimp chips — an important export. Very popular among the Vietnamese, especially at New Year's, they are eaten alone or with hors d'oeuvres. Compared to others, the Vietnamese shrimp cracker has a stronger shrimp taste. Fortunately, it is now made in the United States and is available under the brand name Sa-Giang — an excellent product, much superior to any other. The crackers are raw, however, and must be fried. See Basic Recipes, page 50.

Shrimp Sauce (*mắm ruốc*)

In the Center, shrimp sauce is always added to soups. We also flavor fondues with this condiment. There is no substitute. We have found a Chinese brand to be quite good — Lee Kum Kee. However, if you live in an area where there are Vietnamese groceries, try to get Mắm Ruốc Bā Giáo Thảo, a superior product.

Snow Peas

These are bright green pods, resembling regular pea pods, except that they are flat, with a tiny pea inside. The entire pod is eaten—they are never shelled. Hence in France they are called *pois mange-tout*. Usually sold in Oriental groceries. Fresh, they will keep in the refrigerator for about 2 weeks. They are also sold frozen, but are not crisp this way. If you must use the frozen kind, defrost and blot well to remove any excess water.

Soy Sauce

Same as Chinese thin soy sauce, and "Thin Soy Sauce" will be on the label. Koon Chun is a good brand, easily obtained. If you see "Vietnamese Soy Sauce" on a jar, it is *not* Vietnamese soy sauce; it is a misnomer.

Star Anise

This dried, star-shaped spice, which has eight points or pods, is not frequently used in Vietnamese cooking. However, it is an important flavoring in that dish so dear to the heart of all Vietnamese people —*phở bò hà nội*, or Hanoi Soup (page 52). The spice itself has a licorice flavor, should be stored in a tightly sealed jar, and will keep for several years. It's always available in Oriental groceries. During my last trip to France, I was able to buy some beautiful star anise in the Auvergne.

Straw Mushrooms

In our recipes we use canned straw mushrooms. They have a delicate flavor and are available in Oriental groceries. If not available, substitute small, fresh mushrooms.

Sweet Rice

See Rice.

Tamarind

An acid-flavored fruit, whose pulp and seeds are contained in a large pod resembling a bean pod. The pulp and seeds are usually soaked in water to impart a sour flavor to the water, which is then used in the recipe where it is required. The seeds and pulp are then discarded.

TAMARIND PASTE: It can be purchased, in paste form, in Oriental groceries in a plastic package. Once opened, it should be refrigerated. Keeps indefinitely.

Tapioca Starch

Can be used as a thickener in place of cornstarch. Its most important use in this book is as an ingredient in the preparation of Fresh Rice Papers (page 43).

Tomato Paste

Any brand of French or American tomato paste will do. You'll find a number of recipes calling for tomato paste. After you open the can and remove the amount specified in the recipe, cover the remaining paste with cooking oil and it will keep for a long time in the refrigerator. Whenever a recipe calls for tomato paste, you simply remove the amount called for and cover again with oil.

Tree Ears

Called such in Chinese cookbooks, and we will use the same term because of its familiarity. In Vietnam, however, they are referred to as "cat ear mushrooms." The tree ear is a kind of tree mushroom, sold dried in Oriental grocery stores. Soak at least 20 minutes, then wash and rinse before using. Prized for its crunchy texture, it has no real flavor. Can be stored in a cool, dry place.

Tương

This bears no resemblance to any other sauce. There is no substitute. In the United States, some confusion arises because *tương* is sold in jars labeled "Vietnamese Soy Sauce." It is not Vietnamese soy sauce, but a totally different product. Easily obtainable by mail order from any of the sources in our list or in Vietnamese groceries throughout the United States. One of its many uses is in Nước Lèo (page 35) as well as a substitute for fish sauce (*nước mắm* or Nước Chấm, page 34).

White Radish (*củ cải*)

Similar in taste and appearance to the Western icicle radish, we have used it here as a fast and easy pickled accompaniment to Barbecued Pork (pages 104–5). Available throughout the year at Oriental groceries, it will keep in the refrigerator for several weeks.

Techniques

Fortunately, the techniques common to most Vietnamese recipes are not at all difficult. For convenience, the techniques that are more involved are described in detail in those recipes requiring them.

Frying

In Vietnam we usually use a shallow wok for frying, or an ordinary frying pan — the French influence. Very little oil is used, much less than in Chinese cooking.

STIR-FRYING: Rapid cooking over high heat in a very short period of time. To make things easy, the premeasured ingredients and condiments for any given recipe should be arranged in bowls or on a platter or a tray in the order in which they are to be added to the pan. Oil is added to a preheated wok or frying pan; the food is then added and quickly seared and coated with oil to seal in the juices and retain the natural flavors. All stirring is done with chopsticks, rather than the stirrer or spatula that is used for stir-frying in Chinese cooking. This does not imply that you are forbidden the use of that tool; we are merely educating the reader in Vietnamese matters.

SHALLOW FRYING OR SAUTÉING: In this technique, the frying pan is coated with oil and the food fried over moderate or low heat, long enough to be browned on all sides.

DEEP FRYING: As in all other schools of cooking, whether it be Asian or Western, this is cooking in a large quantity of oil; it is not as important a technique in Vietnamese cooking as it is in Chinese, for example. Any pot can be a deep-fryer, from a wok to a smaller saucepan, depending on how much oil you wish to use and how much food is to be cooked. One must never put too much food into a deep-fryer, as this will reduce the temperature of the oil too drastically. While the oil is returning to the desired temperature, the food tends to absorb the oil and become greasy. If you bear this in mind and cook smaller amounts, you'll always have perfectly fried, crisp food. If you are not sure of your oil temperature, a deep-frying thermometer would be a worthwhile investment. Most deep-fried foods are cooked at about 375 degrees, and with the thermometer you can really control the temperature, raising and lowering the heat as desired.

Barbecuing

In Vietnam, this is an important cooking method. Every home has a small stove made of red clay that is kept on the kitchen floor. The food is barbecued there and brought to the table. There are some dishes that must be barbecued at the table, and for this there is a smaller charcoal stove about the size of a cereal bowl.

In the summer we use our Western-style barbecue grills out of doors, and in the winter we use our ovens. In this book, all foods that are baked in the oven are usually barbecued over charcoal in Vietnam.

Boiling

Cooking a food rapidly in a large amount of water or broth, such as noodles.

Steaming

A steamer consists of a pot in which water is boiled and at least two more metal inserts or layers that fit directly on the lower pot of water, one above the other. These inserts are perforated, allowing wet steam to circulate freely through the layers and enabling either a large quantity of one food or several different foods to be cooked at the same time.

Simmering

Long, slow cooking, in a covered pan, with liquid. Usually cooking time depends on the amount of liquid used and is complete when most of the liquid has evaporated and about ⅓ cup of liquid remains in the pan.

In Vietnam, even the people who own gas stoves feel that simmering over charcoal produces a superior-tasting food. You might want to try that in the summer on your barbecue, but bear in mind that the Vietnamese like charcoal — not compressed briquets.

Making Balls (beef, shrimp, pork)

Chewiness is a much prized quality in Vietnamese cookery. The chewy, flavorful balls of beef, pork or shrimp, are a favorite snack.

In order to develop the necessary firm consistency, place the specified amount of meat in the palm of your hand. Squeeze the meat against your palm with your fingers. Open your hand and the meat will have adhered to the fingers. Using your thumb, roll the meat from your fingers back onto the palm. Repeat 6 times for each ball, then roll into a round ball with both hands.

Basic Recipes

These recipes are grouped in this chapter because they are served with almost all meals or appear very frequently in many recipes. After a while, they will become second nature to the cook.

Vietnamese Sauces

These sauces are an integral part of Vietnamese cuisine, and their importance cannot be overemphasized. *Nước chấm* is very widely used and the others, such as *nước lèo*, ginger fish sauce, and *tương* with ginger are more specific in their accompaniments. However, one characteristic is shared; they enhance and expand the inherent taste of the accompanied dish and do not change it.

Nước Chấm

This exciting sauce is almost always served at Vietnamese meals, just as Westerners serve salt and pepper. Its base is *nước mắm* (bottled fish sauce; see page 16). Freshly prepared, it is a constant delight, and so addictive to Western palates that it will appear with meals other than Vietnamese. To best appreciate the results of its superb blending qualities at the table, use it sparingly at first, gradually adding more until the result is just right for your palate.

Yields 5 tablespoons

1 clove garlic
½ fresh hot red chili pepper or 2 dried
2 heaping teaspoons granulated sugar

⅛ fresh lime
2 tablespoons fish sauce (*nước mắm*)
2½ tablespoons water, more if necessary

Peel the garlic. Split the chili pepper down the center and remove the seeds and membrane. Cut into pieces and put into a mortar, together with the garlic and sugar. Pound into a paste. Squeeze the lime juice into the paste, then with a small knife remove the pulp from the lime section and add it as well. Mash this mixture and add the fish sauce and water.

NOTE

If you find this a trifle strong-tasting at first, dilute it with an additional ½ tablespoon of water.

Nước Lèo

This traditional sauce of the Center, with its unique flavor, blends into many dishes such as Happy Pancake (pages 208–9), Barbecued Beef Wrapped in Fresh Rice Papers (pages 92–93), Barbecued Beef with Lemon Grass and Noodles (page 94), and Barbecued Meatballs (page 69).

Yields 1 cup

1 clove garlic, sliced
1 tablespoon vegetable oil
1 small piece of pork liver (see note below), minced
1 tablespoon ground pork
1 teaspoon tomato paste
¼ cup *tương*
½ cup water

1½ teaspoons peanut butter
1 tablespoon granulated sugar
1½ tablespoons sesame seeds
10 Roasted Peanuts (see page 46), coarsely chopped
Thin strips of hot pepper for garnish (optional)

Using medium heat, fry the garlic in the oil. Add the liver and pork. Lower the heat and add the tomato paste; stir and add the *tương*. Stir again and add the water and peanut butter. Raise the heat to medium and add the sugar. Boil for 1 minute and transfer to a bowl.

Add the sesame seeds to a medium-hot frying pan, stirring constantly until browned. This should take 2 to 3 minutes. Add the sesame seeds to the *nước lèo*, along with the chopped peanuts.

The sauce can be garnished with thin strips of hot pepper.

NOTE

Beef or chicken liver can be substituted, but pork liver is preferred. The piece should be the size of a large chicken liver.

Buddhist Nước Lèo

This sauce is used in Buddhist vegetarian dishes such as Vegetable Spring Rolls (page 161), Buddhist Monk's Soup (page 162), and with any Buddhist dishes.

Yields 6 tablespoons

1 tablespoon granulated sugar
2 tablespoons *tương*
2 tablespoons water

Fresh hot red chili slices to taste (optional)
1 tablespoon Roasted Peanuts (page 46), coarsely chopped

Mix the sugar with the *tương* and water. Add some slices of fresh red chili pepper, if desired, and sprinkle with roasted peanuts.

Ginger Fish Sauce

Nước Chấm Gừng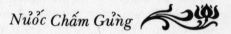

This sauce is served with Duck Rice Soup (page 136).

Yields ¼ cup

2 teaspoons small pieces fresh gingerroot
1 fresh red chili pepper
1 clove garlic

2 teaspoons granulated sugar
5 teaspoons fish sauce (*nước mắm*)
1 tablespoon water
⅛ fresh lime

Put the ginger into a mortar with the red chili pepper, garlic, sugar, and fish sauce. Pound to a paste with the pestle. Squeeze the juice of the lime into the mortar, then remove the pulp of the lime section with a small knife and add it to the paste. Add the water. Mix well.

Tuong with Ginger

 Nước Chấm Tưởng Gừng

This sauce is usually served with Vietnamese roast beef.

Yields ½ cup

3½ teaspoons granulated sugar
2 cloves garlic
1 fresh hot red chili pepper

3 slices fresh gingerroot
3 tablespoons *tưởng*
2 tablespoons water

Put the sugar, garlic, chili pepper, and ginger into a mortar. Crush with the pestle until the sauce becomes smooth, then add the *tưởng* and water. Mix well.

Other Basic Recipes

Basic Vegetable Platter

Diã Rau Sông

A salad or vegetable platter is a very important part of a Vietnamese meal; indeed, it is served at practically every one. The vegetables, which are eaten along with many dishes, are arranged on a platter, and the diner helps himself to whatever he desires. In Vietnam we used many more vegetables and herbs than we can find in the West. But, in spite of that, the following platter makes a satisfactory accompaniment to the dishes we have prepared for this book. All vegetables and herbs are those served in Vietnam, except that the variety is smaller.

8 servings

2 cups soft lettuce leaves (Boston or similar, not iceberg)
1 cup fresh mint leaves
1 cup fresh coriander (Chinese parsley)

1 cup cucumber, peeled in lengthwise strips and with green strips in between, then cut in half lengthwise and into thin horizontal slices, forming semicircles.

🌺 Arrange a mound of lettuce in the center of a platter. Around the lettuce, and touching it, arrange separate mounds of mint and coriander. Arrange the cucumbers in overlapping slices around the complete outer rim of the platter.

This is the basic arrangement of the vegetable platter. On those occasions when a recipe calls for another vegetable, it can be added to this platter.

Carrot Salad

Carot Ngâm Dấm

1 carrot
½ cup water
1 teaspoon vinegar

Pinch of salt
1 teaspoon granulated sugar

Yields ⅓ cup

🌺 Peel the carrot, then, using your peeler, cut long strips of carrot, trying to get as wide a slice as possible, or shred the carrot in a food processor. Take each strip, roll it up tightly, and then cut it into thin strips (similar to cutting noodles.)

Combine the water, vinegar, salt, and sugar. Add the thin carrot strips to the mixture and marinate for at least 15 minutes, or until ready to use. This can be prepared a day ahead. Before using, always drain and discard the liquid.

NOTE

Carrot salad is always added to Nước Chấm (page 34) when it is served with Spring Rolls (pages 58–60).

Carrot and Sweet Radish in Vinegar

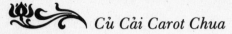 *Củ Cải Carot Chua*

Yields 1 pint

1 medium carrot
1 icicle radish, same size as carrot
1 cup water

2 teaspoons vinegar
2 teaspoons granulated sugar
Dash of salt

To cut the carrot and icicle radish into flower shapes, cut several lengthwise wedges out of each of these vegetables and then slice them paper thin.

Combine the water, vinegar, sugar, and salt in a bowl. Put the vegetables into the marinade for 1 hour before serving. Remove the marinade and serve with dishes like Barbecued Pork with Rice Noodles (pages 104–5).

Pickled Mustard Greens

 *Dủa Cải Chua*

Yields 3 cups

1½ pounds mustard greens
1 bunch scallions
4 cups water

5½ teaspoons salt
1½ teaspoons granulated sugar

Cut the mustard greens and scallions into 2-inch lengths. Wash well and dry in the sun for an entire day, or until the vegetables dry and appear to have shrunk slightly.

Combine the water with the salt and sugar in a large bowl. After the mustard greens and scallions have been dried, transfer them to the bowl of pickling water. Using another bowl or a board as a weight, keep the vegetables submerged in the water.

Cover the bowl and put in a warm place for 3 days. After 3 days, transfer the greens and the liquid to jars and refrigerate. They will keep in the refrigerator for several months.

Serve with Jellied Chicken (page 127), in place of the sour bean sprouts usually served with Pork Simmered with Five Spice Powder (page 108), or with Pork Cooked with Coconut Water (page 106).

Sour Bean Sprouts

Dưa Giá

Usually eaten with Pork Cooked in Coconut Water and Pork Simmered with Five Spice Powder (pages 106, 108).

Yields 3 cups

3 scallions, both green and white
   parts
1 carrot
3 cups water
1 tablespoon salt

½ teaspoon granulated sugar
1 pound bean sprouts
1 tablespoon white vinegar
   (optional; see note below)

Cut each scallion crosswise into 5 pieces. Peel the carrot, then slice it lengthwise with a carrot peeler.

Boil the water, together with the salt and sugar, and cool to room temperature. Put all the vegetables into a large jar and cover with the cooled water. Allow to stand unrefrigerated for 3 days, then transfer to the refrigerator, where the mixture will keep for 4 weeks or longer.

NOTE

When the weather is cool, it is sometimes difficult to start the pickling process. The addition of 1 tablespoon of white vinegar to the water-sugar-salt mixture will help trigger the action.

Perfect Rice

Vietnamese cooks have their own method of measuring the proportions of rice and water. After placing the rice into the pot, they put an index finger on top of the rice, fingertip touching it, and add enough water to reach the first joint.

You will be assured of excellent results if you use the amounts of extra-long-grain rice and water outlined below, as well as the very precise instructions that follow.

1 cup rice	1¾ cups water
2 cups rice	3¼ cups water
3 cups rice	4 cups water

Put the rice and water into a pot and bring the water to a boil over high heat. Continue to boil for about 3 to 4 minutes, or until small holes or craters appear on top of the rice. This is an indication that the water is being absorbed into the rice. While it is actively boiling, cover the pan with a tight lid, thus trapping all the accumulated steam. Reduce the heat to very low immediately. (If the cooking is being done on an electric stove, have a second burner preheated to low, and at this point, after covering, transfer the pot to that low burner.)

Continue to cook over low heat for 20 minutes. After 20 minutes turn off the heat, and without removing the lid allow the rice to rest for an additional 20 minutes. The rice will keep hot for up to 1 hour if the lid remains on. With chopsticks or a fork, stir and fluff the rice.

NOTE

We use no salt in our rice. All the flavoring is in the food with which we serve it. In some recipes we use stock or coconut milk. Follow the same basic procedure as above.

Sweet or Glutinous Rice

Xôi Nếp

In Vietnam we use sweet or glutinous rice very frequently, and often interchangeably with plain rice. Its use in place of plain rice is optional. Tradition dictates when it should be served, but we ourselves feel that there are no hard and fast rules. For example, traditionally some simmered dishes may be served with glutinous rice for breakfast. Never served for lunch, it may be served for dinner with other foods. It is, after all, rice — a little stickier perhaps, but very satisfying and well worth serving.

There are many recipes where we combine other ingredients with glutinous rice—all special-occasion dishes.

Note the proportion of water to rice; as the amount of rice to be cooked increases, the water does not increase in the same way. .

1 cup glutinous rice	2 cups water
2 cups glutinous rice	4 cups water
3 cups glutinous rice	5 cups water

Rinse the rice. Bring the water to a boil and add the rice, leaving the heat at high. Stir once and watch the pot for about 1 minute to make certain the water doesn't boil over. When the water starts bubbling, cover the pot, remove from the heat, and, holding the cover tightly on the pot, drain the water into the sink.

Return the pot to *low* heat, still covered, and cook for 20 minutes. Remove from the heat, uncover, and stir with chopsticks. Or keep it warm for up to an hour over low heat and stir it when you are about to serve.

Fresh Rice Papers

 *Bánh Ướt*   **Yields 20 papers**

1 cup Swansdown cake flour
½ cup tapioca starch
½ cup cornstarch

2½ cups water
2 tablespoons vegetable oil

Combine all the ingredients, stirring with chopsticks or mixing in a blender or food processor. Strain, forcing any solids through the sieve.

Use a 7- or 8-inch frying pan, preferably with a nonstick coating. In order to make sure that this recipe will work well, it is best to preheat your pan for 5 minutes over medium heat. In addition, after each pancake or rice paper is removed from the pan, return the pan to dry over heat for a few seconds before continuing with the next paper. This evaporates any moisture that may have accumulated during steaming.

After preheating for the initial 5 minutes, and keeping the heat at medium, add and swirl 2 tablespoons of batter (enough to cover the bottom of the pan) so it coats the pan. Cover instantly and let the pan remain covered for about 30 seconds; this provides steam. After 30 seconds, remove the cover. If the rice paper is ready to be removed, you will see large bubbles. If none have formed, cover again and cook for a few more seconds. Turn the rice paper out onto an oiled cookie sheet, turning it over from one side to the other until it is well oiled.

Continue cooking the pancakes, periodically stirring the batter to re-combine. They can be cooked ahead and stacked on top of another until needed.

Used in Barbecued Beef with Lemon Grass and Noodles and Rolling Cake recipes (pages 94, 214–15) as a wrapper.

Rice Sticks (for Hanoi Soup)

Bánh Phở

For this recipe we have found that the medium-size rice sticks (¼ inch wide) from Thailand (see page 20) are very good.

8 to 10 servings

To cook 1 bag (1 pound), enough for 8 to 10 people, bring 2 quarts of water to a boil. Drop the noodles in and boil for 4 minutes. Drain in a colander and rinse in cold water.

These noodles can be cooked ahead of time, or just before serving.

Rice Sticks

Bún

These noodles (see page 20) can be cooked ahead of time or just prior to eating.

6 servings

Bring 2 quarts of water to a boil. Drop in ½ pound (½ package) of noodles and return to the boil for 5 minutes.

Drain the noodles in a colander, then rinse under cold water to separate and prevent sticking. Use in recipes where required.

Japanese Alimentary Paste Noodles

 *Somen*

Although these noodles are made of wheat flour, they are a good substitute for rice sticks (*bún*). Bạch has found that to make them as close in every possible way to the noodles she would have been using in Vietnam, they must be cooked very briefly, for just 1 minute. They can be prepared up to 6 hours before serving time, in which case they must be covered.

Each box weighs 1 pound and is divided into 5 ribbon-tied packets. Each packet makes 2 servings. Try to buy the thinnest *somen* available in the store.

To cook a whole box, bring 2 quarts of water to a boil. Drop in the noodles and boil for 1 minute, then transfer to a colander and rinse under cold running water.

NOTE

If you plan to cook them more than 2 hours ahead of time, cover the noodles after they have dried for a while.

Roasted Peanuts

Đậu Phộng Rang

For this we prefer to use peanuts that are shelled but which still have the red inner skin. This prevents scorching of the peanuts as they toast in a hot frying pan.

½ cup shelled peanuts

Heat a dry frying pan until very hot, then add the peanuts and stir constantly until the skins turn black and scorched. Turn into a colander and allow to cool; this takes 2 to 3 minutes. After the peanuts have cooled, squeeze them and rub them together in your hands to remove the skins.

A good technique to learn is the final step in removing the skins. Transfer the peanuts to a colander and shake them up and down. If you get the knack, the skins will fly out of the colander. Of course, it is best to do it over the sink or some place suitable to avoid having the skins all over the floor. If you can't master this technique, it's perfectly acceptable just to rub the skins off. The taste will be the same!

Toasted Sesame Seeds

Mè Rang

Heat a dry frying pan to medium hot. Add sesame seeds and stir constantly until browned. This should take 2 to 3 minutes.

Roasted Rice

 *Thính*

Roasted rice is used quite frequently in Vietnamese cooking. We generally prepare a quantity of it and keep it in a jar to have on hand when needed.

1 cup rice

Heat a small, dry frying pan over high heat and add the rice. Toast, stirring constantly, until the rice is brown. Transfer to a blender and grind into a powder. Store as suggested above.

Caramelized Sugar

Nước Mầu

This brown syrup is used in a number of Vietnamese recipes and is an important ingredient; it is a good idea to prepare it in a larger quantity and keep it on your pantry shelf. Remember not to refrigerate it, as it will harden.

Yields ½ cup

½ cup granulated sugar   1 teaspoon lemon juice
¾ cup water

Put the sugar and ¼ cup of the water into a dry, 8-inch frying pan over high heat. When it starts to brown, start to stir and then stir constantly. When the sugar turns dark brown and you see steam forming, stir well, remove from the heat, and add the remaining ½ cup water. Continuing to stir, return to high heat for about 5 minutes. Add the lemon juice, giving a few quick stirs, and remove from the heat. Allow to cool and transfer to a jar.

If you wish to make a very small amount, enough for one dish, prepare the syrup in a small pan as directed above but using:

1 tablespoon granulated sugar   A squeeze of lemon
¼ cup water

Coconut Milk

 *Nước Cốt Dừa*

Yields 2 cups

In Vietnam, every housewife has her own personal tool designed for removing and grating coconut meat. In the markets, too, after one has selected a coconut, the vendor removes the shell and grates the coconut, using his own specially designed equipment.

Bạch's mother has 4 kinds of coconut in her garden. One is sweet and sour, used for cooking. Another has a lot of water and is sweet, for drinking; the meat is eaten when it is very thin. Still another coconut is very small, about the size of a coffee cup. It grows on a very low tree and the coconut meat as well as the liquid is used. Another type has a green outer shell, which turns red when the meat is thick and ready for cooking or making coconut milk.

To make the coconut milk, hold the coconut over a bowl in a horizontal position in the palm of the hand. With the back of a heavy knife or cleaver, or with a hammer, strike the center of the coconut sharply, rotating the coconut a little each time you strike. You'll probably come back to your starting point a few times, but eventually it will break. The coconut water will pour into the bowl, to be used in such a dish as Pork Cooked with Coconut Water (page 106) or Beef, Shrimp, and Fish Fondue with Coconut Water (pages 186–87).

Remove the coconut meat from the shell, then remove the brown outer skin. Cut the meat into slices and cover with 1½ cups of water. Pour into the blender and blend until very fine, almost a paste. Pour through a strainer; then add water again, about ½ cup, and again strain, squeezing with your hand to extract all the liquid.

This can be stored in the freezer.

Coconut milk is used in Mimosa Rice (pages 194–95), Banana Sweet Soup (page 234), Stuffed Chicken Necks (page 89), and so on.

Stock — chicken, beef, pork

Nủớc cốt gā, bō, heo

   This recipe is for beef, chicken, or pork stock. Many recipes in our book call for stock, and they indicate exactly how much is required for each particular recipe. Our approach is very simple. Using whatever quantity of bones you may have, prepare your stock as follows.

Bring sufficient water to a boil so that when you add the bones and/or meat they will be covered. This will insure a clear stock. Cook uncovered for 15 minutes, skimming frequently. Then cover completely and reduce the heat to medium so it does not boil. (If the heat is too high, the stock will boil and will not be clear.) Cook for a total of 2 hours, then remove and discard the bones.

   Transfer the stock to containers and refrigerate. Freeze if it is to be stored for a longer period of time.

NOTE

We do not add any flavoring to our basic stock because each recipe will have its own.

Shrimp Chips

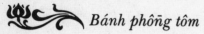 *Bánh phỏng tôm*

These are usually served as an hors d'oeuvre alone or with Cabbage with Meat in the Shape of a Clock (pages 74–75), Vegetables with Meat in a Grapefruit Shell (page 76), and other recipes.

4 ounces (or any amount) raw   1 cup vegetable oil
  shrimp chips (see ingredients,
  page 25)

Heat 1 cup of oil in a small frying pan (the oil should be about 1 inch deep). When the oil is very hot, turn the heat down to medium. Drop in about 3 chips at a time and keep pressing down with chopsticks or a spoon so that they will expand into a larger cracker.

Remove from oil with chopsticks or slotted spoon. Place on paper towels to remove excess oil. The chips cool instantly. They can be eaten at once or stored in a plastic bag for up to a week. They will retain their crunchiness if stored properly.

NOTE

If the oil is too hot, the cracker will not expand sufficiently.

Traditional Vietnamese Favorites

The cuisine of each culture has its hallmark in one or more dishes. In the minds of many, these time-hallowed delicacies are the brilliant jewels in a magnificent mosaic of precious gems. To Vietnamese in foreign lands they represent the memories of their homeland, and to Westerners an unforgettable delight. Truly national dishes, they are served everywhere in Vietnam.

Beef Hanoi Soup
Phở Bò Hà Nội

As you might expect, there is also a Saigon Soup (pages 220–21). However, this is simply a reflection of the pride each region takes in its own specialties. Hanoi Soup has always been a dish of the North. Typically eaten for breakfast (and a hearty breakfast it is!), Hanoi Soup will also be seen on many a luncheon or dinner restaurant menu as well. There are many "breakfast only" restaurants that specialize in Hanoi Soup. Whenever it is served, it constitutes the complete meal.

8 servings

9 cups water
1½ pounds oxtail, chopped into
   2-inch pieces, or 2 pounds of
   beef bones
1 pound beef chuck, in 1 chunk
1 two-inch chunk fresh
   gingerroot
3 shallots
2 star anise
1 finger-size stick cinnamon
   (optional)
¼ cup fresh coriander (Chinese
   parsley), chopped

¼ cup scallion greens, chopped
1 large onion
4 ounces bean sprouts
½ pound beef shoulder roast or
   round, in 1 chunk
½ pound rice sticks (*bánh phở*) (see
   ingredients, page 20)
¼ cup fish sauce (*nước mắm*)
1 teaspoon salt
Dash of MSG (optional)
½ fresh lime, sliced in 4 wedges
½ fresh hot red pepper, sliced
   horizontally in thin rings

Bring 9 cups of water to a boil. Drop in the oxtail and chuck. Return to the boil for 10 minutes, removing the scum several times. Meanwhile, impale the chunk of ginger on a fork and hold it over a flame until it is blackened. Do the same with the shallots. Add both to the broth, together with the star anise and cinnamon, and cover. Simmer for 1½ hours.

While the soup is simmering, chop the Chinese parsley and scallion greens together; place in a bowl. Slice the onion paper thin and place in another bowl.

Blanch the bean sprouts in boiling water for 30 seconds, then remove from the pan.

Slice the round or shoulder roast into paper-thin slices (about 3 × 4 inches).

About 20 minutes before serving, bring 3 quarts of water to a boil and add the rice sticks. Boil for 5 minutes, then drain in a colander and run cold water over. Set aside the noodles until you are ready to assemble the soup.

After the soup has cooked for about 1½ hours, remove the chuck and oxtail, making certain they are tender. If they are not quite ready, return to the soup and cook a little longer. After you have removed the meat from the soup, add the fish sauce, salt, and MSG to the soup.

To assemble and serve the soup, distribute the noodles among the bowls, 1 bowl for each guest. Slice the cooked chuck; remove the meat from the oxtail bones. Distribute the cooked chuck and oxtail meat over the noodles, then distribute the raw beef slices among the bowls. Add half of the onion slices, a few of the bean sprouts, and sprinkle with the combined parsley and scallion greens.

Immediately prior to serving, add boiling broth to cover the ingredients in each bowl. This will cook the raw beef.

At the table, serve a platter consisting of the remaining bean sprouts and onion rings, the lime wedges, and the hot red pepper rings. Serve additional fish sauce for those who prefer a saltier taste. A squeeze of lime can be added to the soup, as well as additional vegetables from the platter, when desired.

NOTE

This can be cooked a day ahead. The meat, wrapped in foil, and the broth should be stored separately in the refrigerator and assembled before serving time. Reheat the meat slightly in the oven before assembling.

Vietnamese New Year Cakes
Bánh Chửng

A charming story is told of a king of ancient Vietnam, when each king was expected to have as many as one hundred wives. Feeling that the time had come for a successor to assume the throne, he called together his many children, announcing that the child preparing the best dish with symbolic meaning would become king. The children thereupon scoured the countryside for rare and expensive delicacies, preparing the most exotic dishes. All, that is, except for his youngest son, who could not afford to buy costly ingredients.

The son prayed day and night for heavenly inspiration. One night, as he slept, God appeared in a dream and told him to prepare a dish of glutinous rice, meat, and mung beans — simple, inexpensive foods — in two shapes, one round and one square, the round shape to symbolize the Universe and the square shape the Earth. After preparing the dish according to the recipe, the youngest child served it to the king. The king was so pleased with this good food — so simple and yet so meaningful — that he gave his throne to the youngest child.

The ingredients in this recipe are usually wrapped in banana leaves, which are not generally available, so we use aluminum foil. The green tint imparted to the rice by the banana leaves can be simulated with green food coloring.

Bánh chửng are usually cooked two days before the New Year. Bạch's mother would make a hundred of these cakes at one time — much larger than those we prepare here. They would be hung in the kitchen and eaten over a two-month period.

Yields 9 cakes

1 pound mung beans, hulled
10 cups sweet or glutinous rice
5 drops green food coloring
   (optional)
8 shallots or white part of 8
   scallions

¼ cup fish sauce (*nước mắm*)
½ teaspoon freshly ground black
   pepper
2½ pounds boneless fresh ham or
   pork shoulder, cut into 2-inch
   squares

In separate bowls, soak the mung beans and sweet rice overnight (12 hours) in enough water to cover. If you wish, add 5 drops of green food col-

oring to the bowl of soaking rice. After 12 hours, drain the rice and the mung beans (still keeping them separate) and allow them to dry in colanders or on paper towels for 2 hours.

While the rice and beans are drying, mash the shallots in a mortar and add the fish sauce and black pepper. Mix well and add to the pork. Marinate for at least 2 hours.

At the end of the marinating time, prepare to wrap and shape the cakes (fig. 1). Cut heavy-duty aluminum foil (18 inches wide) into 20 ten-inch lengths; cut cotton twine into 10 pieces 50 inches long. Spread out a piece of aluminum foil. Place 1 cup of rice on the foil in an approximate 5-inch square. Center, on top of the rice, ¼ cup of mung beans in about a 4-inch square. Put a piece of pork on top of the mung beans, then another ¼ cup of mung beans and another cup of rice. As you keep piling on the ingredients, the top tends to narrow, finally forming a pyramid shape.

Draw the narrow sides of the foil together and make a 1-inch fold, then fold once more to seal. You will still have an excess of foil. Make a fold in it close to where the foil actually touches the rice and place the excess flat along the package. You now have 2 open ends. Fold one end over, thus forming a bag. Stand the package on this closed end and look down into the inside. Shake down the package of rice and add about a handful more of sweet rice to the top; fold over the foil to seal the package well. Turn the package over,

Figure 1

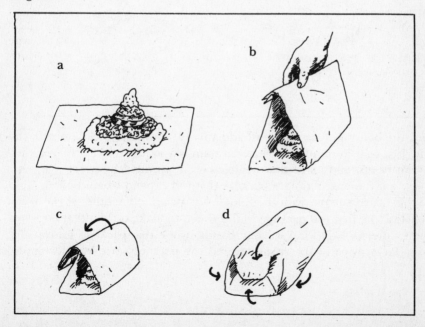

reopen the bottom of the bag, and add a handful of rice; reclose neatly and firmly. Just bear in mind that what you want is a square of meat surrounded by mung beans, and all of that completely surrounded by sweet rice; also, that you want to have a square package that will expand when cooked. Now, place this sealed square, with the folded side down, on another sheet of foil and enclose the first foil package in this sheet, to make certain that no water gets into the package. Using your hands, work this package into a neat square. Tie a piece of the string around the package once lengthwise and

once crosswise, and with the excess string make a loop, to enable the package to be picked up with ease.

Make additional cakes until all the filling is used up.

Place the rice cakes in cold water to cover. Bring to a boil, then cover and continue cooking at a lively boil at medium heat for 6 hours. Check the water level from time to time and replenish with additional water if the level is lower than the rice packages. After 6 hours, remove from the water, cool and refrigerate. The cakes can be kept for several weeks and reheated in the oven or by reboiling.

To serve, cut each cake through the center into 4 squares and eat with Vegetable in Fish Sauce (see below).

VEGETABLE IN FISH SAUCE (*Dưa Món*)

New Year Cake is always served with a combination of green papayas, white radishes, red chili peppers, carrots, white scallions, and small cucumbers, all of which are first dried in the sun and then covered with fish sauce that has been cooked with sugar. After 3 or 4 weeks, it is ready to eat.

In the West vegetables prepared this way are not available; the sun is not hot enough for drying, and the summer is not long enough. Our excellent substitute is "dry sweetened radish," available in a package in Oriental markets. We prefer the tan-colored variety to the dark brown.

Rinse the radish under cold water, then slice. Transfer to a jar and cover with Nước Chấm (page 34).

This can be eaten at once or can be stored in the refrigerator for several months.

Spring Rolls
Chả Giò

Irresistible — gourmets hail them as an inspired creation of an outstanding cuisine — and so they are. Understandably, in Vietnam these crisp-outside, tender-inside, golden-brown delights are served for all occasions — never omitted. They are much smaller and more crisp than the Chinese version. Unlike the Chinese spring roll, they can be rolled in the morning, then covered and refrigerated for several hours before cooking. After cooking, they will keep nice and crisp in a 150-degree oven for up to 3 hours, giving the cook a bit of a breather.

Yields 80 spring rolls

FILLING

2 ounces cellophane noodles, soaked in warm water for 20 minutes, then drained and cut into 1-inch lengths

1 pound ground pork

1 large onion, finely chopped

2 tablespoons tree ears, soaked in warm water for 30 minutes, then drained and finely chopped

3 cloves garlic, finely chopped

3 shallots or white part of 3 scallions, finely chopped

1 can (7 ounces) crabmeat, cartilage removed and meat flaked with fingers

½ teaspoon freshly ground black pepper

PREPARATIONS FOR ASSEMBLING AND FRYING

20 sheets dried rice papers (*bánh tráng*)

4 eggs, well beaten

2 cups peanut oil

ACCOMPANIMENTS FOR SERVING

Basic Vegetable Platter (pages 37–38)

Carrot Salad (page 38)

Double recipe of Nước Chấm (page 34)

🔥 Combine the filling ingredients in a bowl and set aside.

Cut a round rice paper sheet into quarters (fig. 2). Place the cut rice paper on a flat surface. With a pastry brush, paint beaten egg over the entire

surface of each of the pieces. Before filling, wait for the egg mixture to take effect, softening the wrappers; this takes about 2 minutes. When you become adept at this, you can work on several wrappers at a time.

When the wrapper looks soft and transparent, place about 1 teaspoon of filling near the curved side, in the shape of a rectangle. Fold the sides over to enclose the filling and continue to roll.

After filling all the wrappers, pour the oil into a large frying pan, put the spring rolls into the cold oil, turn the heat to moderate, and fry for 20 to 30 minutes, until a lovely golden brown. (This is Bạch's special method of keeping spring rolls crisp.)

Figure 2

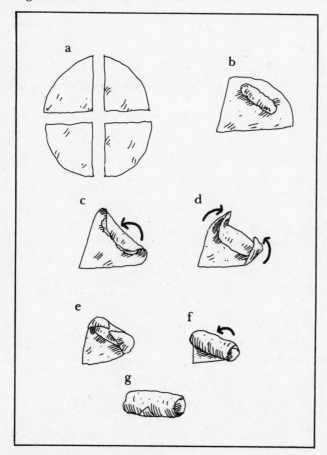

To serve the spring rolls, proceed as follows:

Arrange the ingredients for the vegetable platter (lettuce, mint leaves, coriander, and the cucumber slices) according to the directions on page 38. Have ready the carrot salad and a bowl of *nước chấm*; mix 1 tablespoon of carrot salad into the *nước chấm*. Each person has a bowl into which he places a bit of lettuce, 2 or 3 mint leaves, some coriander, and 2 cucumber slices. Each person then adds 1 or 2 spring rolls to his bowl, sprinkles with *nước chấm*, and eats the spring rolls and vegetables together, using chopsticks or a fork. Additional carrot salad may be added to taste.

Another very popular serving method calls for placing the vegetables on a lettuce leaf, adding the spring roll, and rolling it into a cylinder. Holding the cylinder with his fingers, each diner then dips it into his own small bowl of *nước chấm*.

NOTE

We have found that frying the spring rolls in peanut oil keeps them crisper than frying in any other oil.

Vietnamese Pâtés (*chả*)

In Vietnam, pâtés are rarely, if ever, made at home, although Bach remembers that occasionally her mother's servants would prepare them. These delicacies, so important to the Vietnamese, are always available from special shops that make them daily. In order to prepare them at home in Vietnam, it was necessary to pound for several hours with a heavy stone mortar and pestle. The shopkeepers, on the other hand, had specially designed electric mortars for the manufacture of the pâtés. Here in the West the Vietnamese people have discovered that with the new food processors they can obtain excellent results. If you do not own a food processor, do not attempt these recipes.

There are three basic kinds of pâté, and there are many variations on each of these. For example, the Cinnamon Pâté (page 66) might, in another version, have pork skin and more spices added to it, and a new name, one that the shopkeeper chooses. Our three recipes for the basic pâtés work beautifully — if you follow all the directions, particularly the refrigerating and the brief period of freezing. They are important — and the rewards make the effort worthwhile.

Vietnamese Boiled Pâté
Chả Lụa

This traditional, very versatile food of Vietnam can be served alone, as an appetizer, with drinks, or on French bread as a sandwich. You will find it included as part of several dishes, and we also serve it between 2 sweet rice cakes (see page 216). Usually it is wrapped in banana leaves before cooking, but in the West we use aluminum foil.

Yields 3 six-inch-long pâtés

6 tablespoons fish sauce (*nước mắm*), plus extra for shaping the pâtés
6 tablespoons water
1 tablespoon potato starch or rice flour
½ teaspoon granulated sugar

2 teaspoons baking powder
Dash of MSG (optional)
Sprinkling of freshly ground black pepper
2¼ pounds boneless fresh ham (weight after trimming fat)
4 ounces pork fat

Make a marinade by combining all the ingredients except the fresh ham and pork fat in a large bowl. Remove all the fat from around the ham. Slice the meat ¼ inch thick, then cut into 1-inch squares. Place the sliced meat in the marinade in the large bowl, then mix well with your hands and cover the bowl with plastic wrap or foil and leave in the refrigerator for at least 5 hours or overnight.

Transfer the meat to a freezer for exactly 10 minutes and then grind to a paste in a food processor *only* (see page 8).

Boil the pork fat for 15 minutes and dice into small pieces, about the size of whole peppercorns. Mix the pork fat with the meat paste and divide this into 3 equal parts.

Moisten your hands with water and a little fish sauce (about ¼ teaspoon). Shape each section of the meat mixture into a 6-inch-long sausage shape. You will now execute the typical drugstore wrap, and in order to have a tight seal, you will wrap each package twice.

Cut 6 twelve-inch squares from aluminum foil. Place 1 of the sausages in the center of a piece of aluminum foil (fig. 3). Take the 2 side edges and bring them together. Make a 1-inch fold, then wrap the double layer of foil snugly around the sausage. Fold the sides of the foil to seal the package.

Now, to make the package watertight, repeat the preceding process with a second piece of foil, but start by placing the package fold side down, and then continue in the same way as above. Tie with white kitchen string, once in each direction, in a cross-tie.

Figure 3

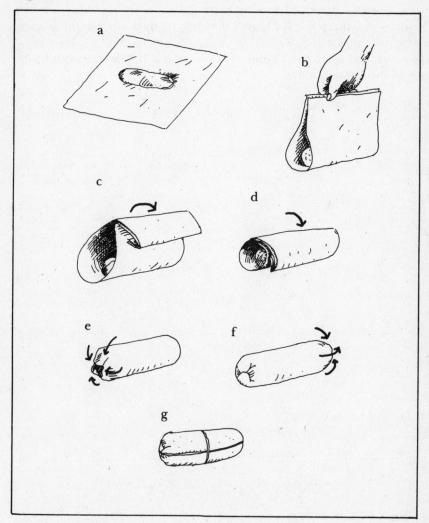

Repeat with the remaining pâtés.

Put into the freezer for exactly 2 hours. After 2 hours have elapsed, remove the packages from the freezer, and place them in a pot and cover with cold water. Turn on the heat to high, bring to a boil, and allow to boil, uncovered, for 40 minutes. (The packages should always be covered with water. Keep checking during the cooking to make certain that they are, and add water if necessary.) Remove from the water.

If you wish to keep this for longer than several days, store in the freezer. Otherwise, refrigerate.

To serve, boil again for 15 minutes or heat in a 350-degree oven for 30 minutes, in the foil wrapping.

Vietnamese Fried Pâté
Chả Chiên

Yields 8 pâtés

6 tablespoons water
6 tablespoons fish sauce (*nước mắm*)
1 tablespoon potato starch or rice flour
½ teaspoon granulated sugar
2 teaspoons baking powder
Dash of MSG (optional)

Sprinkling of freshly ground black pepper
1¼ pounds boneless pork loin (weight after trimming fat)
1 pound of chicken breast (weight after boning and skinning)
Vegetable oil for deep frying

Make a marinade by combining all the ingredients except the pork, chicken, and oil in a large bowl.

Slice the trimmed pork ¼ inch thick, then cut into 1-inch squares. Slice the chicken breast into pieces of similar size. Transfer all the meat to the bowl of marinade, then mix well with your hands and cover with plastic wrap or foil and refrigerate for 5 hours.

After 5 hours, transfer to the freezer for exactly 10 minutes. Grind to a paste in a food processor *only* (see page 8).

·Wet your hands with cold water and, using ⅔ cup of meat for each, shape the meat into round patties, or hamburger-shaped cakes, 1 inch thick.

Using a deep-fryer or any deep saucepan, fill with about 5 inches of oil for deep frying. (This is not to be cooked at the usual deep-fry temperature, which is 375 degrees, but for about 25 to 30 minutes at about 280 degrees. If you have a deep-frying thermometer, it can be very helpful as a guide in maintaining the proper temperature and ensuring good results.) Heat the oil to about 375 degrees and drop in 4 patties at one time. This will immediately reduce the heat to medium, or 280 degrees. Cook the meat, turning the patties several times, using chopsticks. Try to keep the oil temperature at medium heat throughout the cooking. When the meat is a light golden brown and puffed, it is ready and should be removed and drained on a paper towel. Continue cooking the remaining patties.

The pâté will keep fresh in the refrigerator for a week, or for a much longer period in the freezer. To reheat, place the pâté, wrapped in foil, in a 300-degree oven for 15 minutes.

Cinnamon Pâté

Chả Quế

This will keep fresh in the refrigerator for a week, or it can be stored for a longer period in the freezer. To reheat, wrap in foil and place in a 300-degree oven for 15 minutes.

Yields 1 eight-inch-square piece

1 pound boneless pork (weight
  after trimming fat), preferably
  fresh ham
3 tablespoons fish sauce (*nước
  mắm*)
3 tablespoons water
½ tablespoon potato starch
  or rice flour

½ teaspoon granulated sugar
1 teaspoon baking powder
Dash of MSG (optional)
Sprinkling of freshly ground
  black pepper
2 ounces pork fat
½ teaspoon ground cinnamon

Be sure pork is trimmed of all fat. Slice the meat ¼ inch thick, then cut into 1-inch squares. Make a marinade by combining all the remaining ingredients, except for the pork fat and cinnamon, in a large bowl. Add the pork slices to the marinade and mix well with your hands, then cover the bowl with wrap or foil. Refrigerate for 5 hours, and after that period of time has elapsed, transfer the bowl to the freezer for 10 minutes.

Remove the pork from the freezer, add the cinnamon, and reduce to a paste in a food processor *only* (see page 8).

Boil pork fat for 10 minutes and dice into small pieces, the size of whole peppercorns. Add the diced pork fat to the ground pork mixture.

Coat an 8-inch-square baking pan with oil. Put the meat paste into the pan and press down firmly with your hands, making sure the surface is smooth. The meat will come halfway up the side of the pan.

Preheat the oven to 350 degrees and bake the pâté for 40 minutes, or until the surface looks brown. Remove from the oven and allow to cool. Then slice and serve as an appetizer or with French bread for lunch or dinner, or use in any recipe where it is required. It can be eaten hot or cold.

Shrimp on Sugar Cane

Chạo Tôm

Although you can make this in a food processor or blender, it's best to pound it in a mortar with a pestle to achieve that certain crunchiness which is a most desirable quality of much Vietnamese food. Bạch started using a mortar and pestle when she was thirteen years old, working with a pestle that was about a yard long and 5 inches in diameter. Although her family had many servants, her mother, a great cook, wanted Bạch to learn to use this tool properly. And Bạch, who loved to cook as much then as she does now, was a willing and eager student.

In Vietnam, where this is a very important dish, both the sugar cane and shrimp, fresh from the sea, are brought to the door by the country people. If you cannot obtain sugar cane, you can prepare this dish with crab claws instead (see page 152).

In the West, we have been baking this in the oven. Originally it was barbecued over charcoal, and if you wish you can do the same. Just cook it for 10 minutes on each side and this attractive dish will be reproduced exactly as it is in Vietnam.

6 servings

1 pound raw shrimp in shell
4 cloves garlic
1 teaspoon rock sugar, pounded to a powder, or 1 teaspoon granulated sugar
2 egg whites, beaten until slightly frothy
1 tablespoon Roasted Rice Powder (page 23)
Sprinkling of freshly ground black pepper

2 tablespoons pork fat, boiled for 10 minutes and diced very small
1 twelve-inch section sugar cane
¼ cup vegetable oil, approximately
Basic Vegetable Platter (pages 37–38)
12 dried rice papers (*bánh tráng*)
Nước Lèo with Tamarind (see page 68)

Shell and devein the shrimp, then rinse. Dry thoroughly in paper towels, blotting many times.

Mash the garlic in a mortar, then add the shrimp, a few at a time, and mash to a paste. If the mortar is not large enough, it will be necessary to remove the already prepared shrimp paste to make room for the additional shrimp to be pounded. After all the shrimp is reduced to a smooth paste, pound the sugar into the shrimp, then add the egg white and pound with the pestle until well blended. Finally add the roasted rice powder, black pepper, and pork fat, combining all the ingredients.

Peel the sugar cane. Cut into 4-inch lengths and then split lengthwise into quarters.

Pour about ¼ cup of oil into a bowl. Dip your fingers into the oil and pick up about 2 tablespoons of shrimp paste. Mold it into an oval, around and halfway down the sugar cane, leaving half of the sugar cane exposed to serve as a handle. Proceed until you have used up all the shrimp paste.

Preheat the oven to 350 degrees. Put the shrimp on sugar cane on a baking sheet, then bake for 30 minutes or until brown. Serve with the vegetable platter, dried rice papers, and *nước lèo* with tamarind, as follows:

Each person is given a dried rice paper, and, dipping his finger in water, he moistens the entire surface of the paper, which soon becomes soft and flexible. He then helps himself, from the vegetable platter, to some lettuce, cucumber, coriander, and mint, if available. Then he takes a sugar cane stick, removes the shrimp patty, breaks it in half lengthwise, and places it on top of the vegetables, all in a cylinder, at one end of the rice paper. Then he folds over each side to enclose the filling and rolls it up. Holding it in his hand, he then dips it in his own small bowl of sauce.

While you eat the shrimp in rice paper, you can also chew on the sugar cane.

NƯỚC LÈO WITH TAMARIND

1 tablespoon tamarind paste	1 teaspoon granulated sugar
½ cup plus 3 tablespoons water	2 tablespoons peanut butter
1 tablespoon vegetable oil	2 tablespoons Roasted Peanuts
2 cloves garlic, chopped	(page 46)
⅓ cup *tương*	

Soak the tamarind paste in the 3 tablespoons water.

Heat the oil and add the chopped garlic; cook briefly. Add the water from the tamarind to the saucepan, discarding the remaining tamarind paste and seeds. Stir and add the *tương*, ½ cup water, sugar, peanut butter. Mix well and boil for 2 minutes, stirring constantly. Sprinkle the nuts on top of the sauce and pour into individual bowls for serving.

Barbecued Meatballs

Nem Nướng

6 servings

1 pound fresh ham (weight after
  trimming fat)
2 cloves garlic, chopped
2 shallots or white part of 2
  scallions, chopped
½ teaspoon salt
½ teaspoon pulverized rock sugar
  or granulated sugar
Sprinkling of freshly ground
  black pepper

2 tablespoons Roasted Rice
  Powder (page 23)
2 ounces pork fat, boiled for 10
  minutes and diced
Nước Lèo (page 35)
Dried rice papers
Basic Vegetable Platter (pages
  37–38)

Cut the pork into pieces 1 inch square and ½ inch thick. Combine with the garlic, shallots, salt, sugar, and pepper and marinate for at least 2 hours.

Using a large mortar and pestle or a food processor, reduce this meat to a paste. Transfer to a bowl and add the rice powder and pork fat. Shape into balls, using 1 tablespoon meat for each.

Skewer the meatballs and barbecue over charcoal (medium heat) for 15 minutes on each side until browned, or bake in a 300-degree oven for 15 minutes on each side.

When ready to serve, give each person 3 dishes — a flat plate on which to place the dried rice paper, a bowl of water, and a small dish of *nước lèo*. Using the fingers, each diner then paints the entire surface of a rice paper with water. In about 2 minutes the rice paper will become pliable. A piece of lettuce, cucumber, coriander, and mint (if available) from the vegetable platter should be placed on the rice paper, along with 3 meatballs, then the sides folded over and rolled. The roll is then picked up, dipped in the *nước lèo*, and eaten.

Beef Balls
Bò Viên

As apple pie is American, so beef balls are Vietnamese. Truly a national dish, beef balls, along with pâté, are one of the first foods manufactured by and for Vietnamese when they are transplanted to a foreign country. Loved by everyone, children as well as the most sophisticated gourmet, beef balls can be a main course for dinner or an after-dinner snack. In Vietnam, there are restaurants that serve only beef balls. As Bạch says, "Since we came to the United States, I have been cooking this. My family loves the way it crunches in our mouths."

If you do not have a food processor, this dish must be prepared with a mortar and pestle. It has to be pounded to a paste and neither a blender nor a meat grinder can do this job.

8 servings

BEEF BALLS

6 tablespoons fish sauce (nước mắm)
6 tablespoons water
1 heaping tablespoon potato starch
½ teaspoon granulated sugar
2 teaspoons baking powder

⅛ teaspoon freshly ground black pepper
Dash of MSG (optional)
2 tablespoons Oriental sesame oil
2 pounds 3 ounces boneless beef round (weight after trimming fat)

STOCK

Broth remaining from beef balls
2 teaspoons fish sauce (nước mắm)
½ teaspoon salt

Dash of MSG (optional)
½ teaspoon preserved vegetable (tân xại)

ACCOMPANIMENTS FOR SERVING

Chopped scallion greens
Black pepper

Chili paste with garlic (optional)

Combine, in a large bowl, the fish sauce, water, potato starch, sugar, baking powder, black pepper, and optional MSG.

Set the sesame oil aside in a small bowl.

Weigh the meat to make certain the weight is exactly 2 pounds 3 ounces after trimming, then cut into thin slices approximately 2 inches square. Transfer the meat to the bowl containing the fish sauce and other flavorings. Mix well with your hands, cover with plastic wrap or foil, and refrigerate for at least 5 hours.

After the meat has marinated for the 5 hours, it must be reduced to a very smooth paste. This can be done in either a food processor (half a pound at a time) or in a mortar with a pestle.

Using the reserved sesame oil, rub some on your hand (right or left), and make balls, using 1 tablespoon of meat for each and shaping all of the meat into balls.

Bring 2 quarts of water to a boil over high heat and drop in the beef balls. After they float to the surface, continue to boil for 5 minutes more, then remove from the water, reserving the water for the stock.

Combine all the ingredients for the stock with the beef broth. Reheat the broth when ready to serve, then drop in the beef balls and cook just long enough to reheat.

To serve, place 4 or more beef balls into each soup bowl, along with ⅓ cup of broth, then sprinkle on some chopped scallion greens and a little black pepper. Serve with chili paste with garlic on the side if desired.

NOTE

Both the beef balls and the broth can be frozen in separate containers and used as desired. Chili paste with garlic is available in Oriental groceries.

Appetizers

Fascinating in their diversity, appetizers, with their alternating powerful, subtle, spicy and hot flavors and crunchy textures, offer a bewildering array of choices. Certain rules are followed. When appetizers appear as part of a formal meal, they are served only as a first course — as an accompaniment with drinks — and the guests must be seated. On occasion, but never at a family affair, cocktail parties are held with many guests. At these affairs, appetizers and other foods easy to manage while standing are served. We include appetizers in other chapters as well (see Index).

Cabbage with Meat in the Shape of a Clock

Gỏi Đồng Hồ

An hors d'oeuvre served at parties. Bach learned to make this beautiful dish from her famous teacher in Saigon, Mme. Quốc Việt.

8 servings

6 ounces pork butt
1 chicken leg with thigh
2 ounces raw shrimp, in shell
½ pound outer leaves of cabbage
2 cucumbers
1 large carrot
1 small onion
1 tablespoon distilled white vinegar
2 eggs
1 teaspoon all-purpose flour

Pinch of salt
Sprinkling of freshly ground black pepper
1 clove garlic, chopped
1 teaspoon vegetable oil
5 tablespoons Nước Chấm (page 34)
2 tablespoons Roasted Peanuts (see page 46), coarsely chopped
4 ounces Shrimp Chips (page 50)

Put the pork and chicken into a saucepan and cover with water. Boil, uncovered, for 20 minutes, then cool. Cut the pork into thin strips; you'll find it's easier to pull the chicken into shreds with your hands.

Cook the shrimp in ½ cup water for 3 minutes; drain, then peel and devein and cut into thin strips.

Remove the hard center portion of each cabbage leaf, then shred very fine, as for coleslaw.

Try to remove the skin from both cucumbers in 1 piece. Shred the skin of 1 horizontally; reserve the remaining skin for cutting the numbers and hands of the "clock." Save the cucumber meat for another purpose.

Peel the carrot; slice very thin with a carrot peeler, lengthwise, then roll each slice up very tightly. Starting at either open end, slice each roll into thin strips.

Slice the onion in half, then into thin crosswise slices. Sprinkle on the tablespoon of vinegar and let stand.

Beat the eggs with the flour, salt, black pepper, and garlic. Heat the oil in an 8-inch frying pan until very hot. Add the beaten egg, making sure it covers the bottom of the pan. Cook on one side, then turn over and cook on the other side until slightly brown. Remove and set aside.

In a bowl, combine all the shredded vegetables with the shrimp and meats. Stir well with the *nước chấm*, then stir further and add the marinated onions and peanuts. Press the mixture into an 8-inch round cake pan. Cover with a serving plate, then invert and turn the mixture onto the plate. Place the egg pancake over the vegetable-meat circle.

Cut the remaining cucumber skin into the numbers and hands of a clock. Arrange all of these over the egg pancake and point the hands to the dinner hour.

Serve as a spread on shrimp chips.

Vegetables with Meat in a Grapefruit Shell
Nộm Trái Bưởi

The thick-skinned, easy-to-peel grapefruit in Vietnam are at least twice as large as those in the West, and there is a sour as well as a sweet grapefruit. In this recipe, we use the American grapefruit as a substitute. Weary dieters will find this dish a most welcome change.

8 servings

1 medium onion
Distilled white vinegar
2 cups bean sprouts
4 ounces pork butt
1 large carrot
Skin of 1 large cucumber
2 ounces raw shrimp, in shell

1 small dried squid
2 tablespoons sesame seeds
Nước Chấm (page 34)
1 large grapefruit
1 long, fresh hot red chili pepper
Shrimp Chips (page 50)

Slice the onion in half lengthwise; cut across in paper-thin horizontal slices. Cover with distilled white vinegar for 20 minutes, then drain and discard the vinegar. Squeeze the onion dry with your hands.

Plunge the bean sprouts into boiling water and drain immediately.

Boil the pork for 20 minutes, then drain and cut into thin slices and then into long, narrow strips; cut the carrot and cucumber skin into strips the same size as the pork. Boil the shrimp for 3 minutes; shell and devein, then shred.

Toast the dried squid in the broiler until slightly brown, or over an open flame in a wire broiler. Remove from the heat and pound with the back of a knife to tenderize. Shred the squid with your hands, just pulling it apart.

Toast the sesame seeds (see Basic Recipes, page 46).

Combine all the preceding ingredients and add the *nước chấm* to them, mixing well.

Remove and discard the top of the grapefruit and scoop out the pulp. Add 3 tablespoons of the pulp to the meat and vegetable mixture, then fill the empty grapefruit shell with it.

Slice the chili pepper vertically into 8 sections, without cutting through to the stem, to simulate a flower and decorate the grapefruit shell by sticking the chili pepper into the top.

Serve as a spread on shrimp chips.

Cabbage with Meat and Dried Jellyfish

Gỏi Sứá Khô

The contrasting textures of the crisp cabbage, meat, and chewy jellyfish, spiked with vinegared onion, make this a real appetite teaser.

8 servings

1 piece dried jellyfish, the size of a
   hand
2 chicken legs with thighs
6 ounces boneless pork shoulder
   or fresh ham
1 small cabbage
1 small onion
Distilled white vinegar
2 tablespoons chopped fresh mint
   leaves

2 tablespoons chopped fresh
   coriander (Chinese parsley)
5 tablespoons Nước Chấm (page
   34)
20 Roasted Peanuts (page 46),
   pounded into coarse chunks in
   a mortar
4 ounces Shrimp Chips (page 50)

Soak the jellyfish in hot water for at least 30 minutes.

Bring water to a boil. Drop in the chicken legs and pork and cook at a lively boil for 20 minutes. While the meat is cooking, remove the outer leaves from the cabbage and discard. Remove the hard seams from the remaining cabbage leaves, then shred the cabbage very fine. Slice the onion paper thin. Marinate it in distilled white vinegar for 10 minutes.

Remove the chicken and pork from the water. Slice the pork, then shred it into strips and add to the cabbage. Tear the chicken apart into long strips and add to the cabbage. Add the mint leaves to the cabbage.

Remove the jellyfish from the hot water, wash, then shred, not too fine, and add to the cabbage. Remove the onion from the marinade, then add to the cabbage; add the coriander to the cabbage. Add the *nước chấm* to the cabbage mixture and transfer to a serving platter. Sprinkle the peanuts on top and serve with the shrimp chips.

Meat-Stuffed Squid

Mực Nhồi Thịt

Fried or steamed, this hors d'oeuvre will be an instant success. The resilient texture of the squid and the tasty filling are a favorite with or without drinks—a real winner.

6 servings

12 small squid
¾ pound ground pork
1 large clove garlic, chopped
2 shallots or white part of 2
 scallions, chopped
¼ teaspoon black pepper

1½ teaspoons fish sauce (*nước
 mắm*)
¼ teaspoon granulated sugar
¼ teaspoon salt
Vegetable oil for frying

Wash the squid, 1 at a time, under cold running water. Remove and discard the thin, purplish outer skin by rubbing with your hand as you wash; the skin will peel away. Cut off the tentacle clusters and reserve 5; remove the heads and plasticlike cartilage from the center of the body and discard. (This leaves the long, narrow body, which can then be stuffed.)

After you have washed the squid well, set them aside to dry in a colander for about 20 minutes. Using a paper towel, pat each one dry both on the inside and outside.

Combine the meat with the garlic and shallots, then sprinkle black pepper, fish sauce, sugar, and salt over the mixture; this makes the meat very firm and crunchy. Working with your hands, mix very well. Chop the 5 reserved tentacle clusters very fine and add to the meat.

Stuff each squid with the meat mixture, using your finger or a chopstick to force the meat all the way to the tip of the squid. Stuff the squid two-thirds full, to leave room for swelling during the cooking process.

Heat enough oil over a high flame in a frying pan or wok to reach ½ inch up the side of the pan. Drop the stuffed squid in and reduce the heat to medium. Turn the squid several times to coat with oil and allow them to cook, uncovered, for about 20 minutes without turning. Turn up the heat to brown the squid, then turn them over and cook for another 10 minutes.

Serve with Carrot and Sweet Radish in Vinegar (page 39), rice, and Nước Chấm (page 34).

NOTE

The stuffed squid can also be steamed. Place squid on a platter, then put into a steamer over high heat (see page 30) and steam for 30 minutes. This can be cooked several hours ahead of time and resteamed at serving time, just long enough to get hot.

Dried Jellyfish with Cucumber

Gỏi Sứa Tôm Thịt

6 servings

1 piece dried jellyfish (about the
size of a hand)
1 large cucumber, unpeeled
Salt
2 ounces pork butt
4 ounces small shrimp
1 tablespoon vegetable oil
1 shallot or white part of 1
scallion, chopped

Sprinkling of freshly ground
black pepper
1 teaspoon fish sauce (*nước mắm*)
3 tablespoons chopped Roasted
Peanuts (page 46)
Sprig of fresh coriander (Chinese
parsley) for garnish

Soak the dried jellyfish in hot water for 2 hours.

Cut the cucumber in half lengthwise; remove the seeds with a spoon. Slice paper thin, then place in a bowl and sprinkle on 1 teaspoon salt. After 10 minutes, rinse under cold water. Squeeze with your hands to remove all liquid and set aside.

Cut pork into thin slices and then into thin strips. Peel the shrimp, then clean, wash, and set aside to dry for a few minutes. Cut the soaked jellyfish into thin strips.

Heat the oil in a frying pan. Add the chopped shallot and cook, stirring, for 1 minute, then add the pork and shrimp. Cook and stir for 5 minutes, then add the black pepper, a sprinkling of salt, and the fish sauce. Stir for 3 more minutes. Add the cucumber, roasted peanuts, and jellyfish. Stir well, remove at once, and transfer to a platter.

Decorate with a sprig of fresh coriander and serve with Shrimp Chips (page 50), as an appetizer.

Bamboo Shoots with Shrimp and Meat

Gỏi Măng Tôm Thịt

This dish, a Center dish, can be eaten as a snack or as a first course with drinks. It can be served hot or at room temperature with shrimp chips.

8 servings

1 can (5 ounces) bamboo shoots
4 ounces pork, thinly sliced
4 ounces raw shrimp, shelled and
   deveined
1 tablespoon vegetable oil
1 clove garlic, chopped
2 shallots or white part of 2
   scallions, chopped
2 teaspoons fish sauce (*nước mắm*)

Sprinkling of freshly ground
   black pepper
2 tablespoons Toasted Sesame
   Seeds (page 46)
3 tablespoons Roasted Peanuts
   (page 46), chopped
1 tablespoon chopped fresh mint
   leaves
4 ounces Shrimp Chips (page 50)

Slice the bamboo shoots ⅛ inch thick, then cut into strips about ¼ inch wide; shred the pork into thin strips. Cut the shrimp in half and then into strips.

Heat a frying pan over high heat and add the oil. Fry the garlic and shallots, then add the pork; keep stirring until there is no trace of pink visible. Add the shrimp, then the bamboo shoots; stir well to combine. Add the fish sauce and black pepper, then the sesame seeds, chopped peanuts, and chopped mint leaves. Mix well and transfer to a serving platter.

Serve either immediately, hot, or several hours later at room temperature, with the shrimp chips. (The diner helps himself to a chip and then fills it with the bamboo-pork mixture.)

Lettuce Roll with Shrimp, Meat, and Noodle
Cuốn Diếp

These light, aromatic little packages, with their scallion-green ties, grace every Vietnamese hors d'oeuvre table.

6 servings

4 ounces rice sticks (*bún*) or 1 packet Japanese alimentary paste noodles (*somen*)
½ pound raw shrimp, in shell
½ pound boneless pork loin or chops

½ cup coriander (Chinese parsley)
1 bunch scallions, green part only
1 head Boston lettuce
½ cup mint leaves

Boil the noodles (see Basic Recipes, page 44 or 45); set aside.

Boil the shrimp for 5 minutes, then shell, devein, and cut in half lengthwise.

Boil the pork for 20 minutes in water to cover, then remove from the water and slice thinly into 1 × 2-inch pieces.

Remove and discard the heavy part of the stems from the coriander, then cut into 3 crosswise sections. Plunge the scallion greens into boiling water and remove immediately. Cut each lettuce leaf in half through the center vein.

Place, on the narrow end of each piece of lettuce, 1 slice of pork, 1 piece of shrimp, 1 tablespoon of noodles, 2 mint leaves, and 2 pieces of coriander and roll into a cylinder shape. Tie a scallion green around the center of each lettuce roll to prevent unrolling, then trim each side with a knife to make it look neat and attractive when arranged on a platter.

Serve with Nước Chấm (page 34).

Crab Fried with Salt

Cua Rang Muối

4 servings

2 large hard-shelled crabs or 1
  pound crab claws
2 tablespoons vegetable oil

3 cloves garlic, chopped
2 teaspoons tomato paste
Salt to taste

Clean the whole crabs, if using, in cold water. Twist and remove the skirt attached to the underside of each, then remove the spongy parts attached to the interior and discard. Pull away and discard the top shell. Wash and dry the crab bodies and chop each one in half. Crack the claws with a heavy knife.

In a frying pan, heat the oil over a high flame. Add the garlic and stir for 1 minute; do not allow the garlic to burn. Add the tomato paste and stir for 1 minute longer, then add the crab and sprinkle with salt. Cover, turn the heat down to medium, and cook for 5 minutes.

Uncover and stir a few more times, then remove from the heat and transfer to a platter. Serve at once.

NOTE

This is finger food, and traditionally, after the crabs have been eaten, hands are cleaned with a squeeze of lime and a rinse in a warm cup of tea.

Triangle Spring Rolls

Ram Cuốn

8 servings

½ pound ground beef
1 cup bean sprouts
½ small onion, minced
1 ounce cellophane noodles,
soaked for 20 minutes, then
drained and cut into 1-inch
pieces
2 shallots or white part of 2
scallions, chopped
2 cloves garlic, chopped

Sprinkling of freshly ground
black pepper
4 ounces crabmeat, cooked and
flaked
8 whole dried rice papers
2 eggs, beaten
8 raw shrimp, shelled but with tail
sections attached
2 cups vegetable oil
Vegetable platter
Nước Chấm (page 34)

Make a filling by combining the beef, bean sprouts, onion, cellophane noodles, shallots, garlic, pepper, and crabmeat. Set aside.

Place the dried rice papers on a flat surface. Handling 1 paper at a time, paint the entire surface with beaten egg. Allow to soften for a few seconds. Fold one-third of the rice paper over; this will result in a kind of semicircle with 1 straight edge (fig. 4).

Figure 4

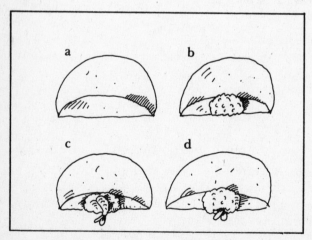

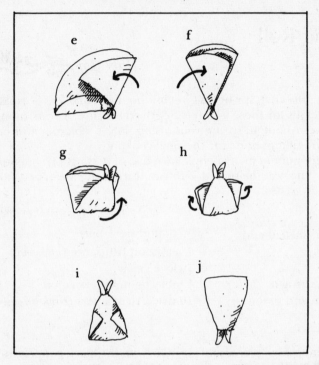

Place 2 tablespoons of the filling on the paper, centering it along the straight edge and shaping the filling into a 2-inch square. Place the shrimp on the filling, leaving the tail section extended to serve as a handle. Place an additional 2 tablespoons of filling on top of the shrimp, then fold the sides over to enclose the filling, forming a point where the shrimp tail extends. Fold over in half toward the curved part. The tail should extend 1 inch over the curved edge. Bring the remaining sides over to the back and tuck in any ragged edges. The egg-coated wrapper will hold together. The completed spring roll should resemble a triangle with a handle.

After filling all the rice papers, pour the oil into a large frying pan, put the spring rolls into the cold oil, turn the heat to moderate, and fry for about 30 minutes, until golden brown.

To serve, place on the table a vegetable platter and a bowl of *nước chấm*. Each person has a bowl into which he places a piece of lettuce, 2 or 3 mint leaves, some coriander, and a few cucumber slices. To this he adds a triangle spring roll, sprinkles on some *nước chấm* and eats the spring roll with the vegetables, using the shrimp as a handle.

Square Spring Roll

Ram Gói

Here is a wonderfully crisp spring roll, yet it is not fried in oil, as is usual. It's particularly marvelous for those who feel deprived because of restrictions in their diets. Imagine! About 40 spring rolls, using only 1 tablespoon of oil — and that just for the filling; none for the final cooking.

In Vietnam, where not too many people own ovens, these are frequently baked over charcoal. They can be served with rice during the meal, or as an hors d'oeuvre.

10 servings

½ pound raw shrimp, shelled and deveined
Black pepper
½ teaspoon granulated sugar
2 scallions, both white and green parts

½ pound pork butt
1 teaspoon fish sauce (*nước mắm*)
1 clove garlic
1 tablespoon vegetable oil
10 dried rice papers (*bánh tráng*)

Cut the shrimp into small pieces and sprinkle with the black pepper and the sugar. Slice the scallions crosswise into very thin slices. Slice the pork into thin pieces, 3 × 2 × ⅛ inches.

Combine half the sliced scallion with the shrimp and meat, the fish sauce, and a dash of black pepper.

Chop the garlic fine; place on a platter near the stove, along with the remaining scallion.

Heat the oil and fry the garlic and remaining scallion briefly until they brown slightly. Add the pork-shrimp mixture and keep stirring over high heat until cooked, about 5 minutes.

Cut or break the 10 rice papers into quarters. Place the cut rice papers on a flat surface. Using a pastry brush, or your fingers, paint water over the entire surface of each of the pieces; this is to make the brittle papers become soft and flexible. Try working on about 10 quarters at a time. This will help you to work faster. While some of the wrappers become pliable, you can be filling the others.

Place 2 pieces of shrimp and 2 small pieces of pork on the pointed end of a paper, arranging the filling in a square shape. Bend the pointed end

over the filling and roll twice, then fold the sides over and continue to roll into a 2-inch-long cylinder about 1 inch thick. Place on a tray, with the open end on the underside to prevent unrolling, while you fill the remaining rolls. Place the rolls in the oven, directly on the oven rack, without preheating. (They can be crowded together while baking so that you can get many onto 1 rack.) Again, be certain to place them open end down; turn the oven to 350 degrees and bake them approximately 40 minutes, 20 minutes on each side.

NOTE

These can be filled several hours before cooking, covered with a plastic wrap, and refrigerated. Or they can be baked and then kept at room temperature for several hours. They never lose their crispness. Use bamboo chopsticks or tongs for turning the rolls.

Golden Coins

Kim Tiền Kê

4 to 8 servings

1 whole chicken breast, skinned
  and boned
½ pound boiled ham, cut into
  ¼-inch slices
2 Chinese sausages
1 teaspoon granulated sugar
½ teaspoon five spice powder

½ teaspoon freshly ground black
  pepper
2 tablespoons black soy sauce
1 tablespoon oyster sauce
  (optional)
¼ cup dry white wine

Cut the chicken breast and ham into 1-inch squares; cut the sausages into slices ¼ inch thick. Marinate all the meat in the remaining ingredients for at least 30 minutes.

Skewer the meat, alternating the chicken, ham, and sausages, and barbecue over the charcoal until the meat is slightly browned.

Serve as an appetizer or with cooked glutinous rice as an entire meal.

Stuffed Chicken Necks Cooked in Coconut Milk

Cổ Gà Dồn Thịt

Permeated with the warm, gentle flavor of coconut milk, these delectable morsels are frequently served as appetizers with drinks or as part of a complete meal.

6 servings

½ pound ground pork
½ small onion, chopped
3 tablespoons chopped canned
 button mushrooms
2 shallots or white part of 2
 scallions, chopped
2 cloves garlic, chopped
Sprinkling of freshly ground
 black pepper

¼ cup green peas, fresh or frozen
1½ teaspoons fish sauce (*nước
 mắm*)
½ teaspoon granulated sugar
4 chicken necks
2 tablespoons vegetable oil
1 cup coconut milk, fresh (see
 page 48) or canned

In a bowl, combine the ground pork, onion, mushrooms, shallots, garlic, and black pepper.

Boil the peas in salted water for 5 minutes, then drain and add, along with the fish sauce and sugar, to the meat mixture. Mix well with your hands.

Remove the bones from each of the chicken necks and discard or reserve for stock. Sew the narrow ends of the neck skins to make casings. Stuff the skins with the pork mixture, then sew up the wider ends. Check the entire skin to make sure there are no tears, or the filling will seep out while cooking. If there are any tears, sew them closed.

Heat the oil in a small saucepan. Add the stuffed chicken necks and brown well on all sides. After the necks are well browned, pour off the oil remaining in the pan. Return to the heat, and pour in coconut milk to cover. Simmer, covered, until all the liquid has evaporated. (If liquid has not evaporated after 30 minutes, uncover, turn the heat to high, and reduce the liquid in this way.)

Remove the necks from the pan. Pull out the threads and discard. Allow the necks to cool for a little while, then cut into ¼-inch slices.

Pickled Pigs' Ears

Tai Heo Ngâm Chua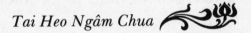

Lip-smacking, tangy, chewy, and exotic, these morsels go perfectly with drinks before dinner, and very well without drinks at any time.

Yields 2 quarts

4 quarts water	2 cups granulated sugar
1 tablespoon alum	1 teaspoon salt
2 cups distilled white vinegar	2 pounds pigs' ears

Boil 2 quarts of the water with the alum for 5 minutes, then remove from the heat and allow to cool.

Boil the vinegar with the sugar and salt for a few minutes, or until the sugar is completely dissolved. Remove from the heat and cool.

Boil the remaining 2 quarts water and drop in the pigs' ears. Boil for 20 minutes. Remove the pigs' ears and cut them into lengthwise slices ¼ inch wide. After the sliced pigs' ears have cooled, return them to the alum water to soak for 2 hours, then drain and rinse under cold water. Dry lightly.

Place the pigs' ears in a jar, pressing them down. Pour in enough cooled vinegar mixture to completely cover the contents of the jar. Refrigerate.

NOTE

This can be eaten after 3 days and will keep for several weeks in the refrigerator.

Beef

Vietnamese beef is of very good quality. It is brought to market immediately after slaughtering and is never refrigerated. One generally buys the fresh-killed beef daily from one's favorite dealer.

The shortage of land for grazing cattle on a large scale keeps beef prices high. Consequently, beef is generally seen on the tables of wealthier families.

Barbecued Beef Wrapped in Fresh Rice Papers
Bánh Ướt Thịt Nướng

These tangy morsels of beef, studded with sesame seeds and wrapped in soft white rice papers, are a highly esteemed party dish. Arranged on a platter like the spokes of a wheel, they are decorative as well as delicious. Prepare them in quantity; once tasted, they will disappear as fast as they are placed on the table.

In Vietnam, the fresh rice papers are purchased in the market. There they are small, about 6 inches in diameter, and especially thin — a ½-inch stack usually contains about 100 rice papers! Fortunately, they are easy to prepare (see page 43), and it is by no means necessary to make them that thin.

We have given instructions for baking the beef, but it can also be barbecued over charcoal—or broiled in the oven—2 minutes on each side.

Note that if you are using dried lemon grass, you must allow 2 hours for it to soak before you start the recipe.

8 servings

MARINADE

2 stalks fresh lemon grass or 2
   tablespoons dried lemon grass
2 cloves garlic
1 tablespoon granulated sugar
3 shallots or scallions (white part
   only)

1 tablespoon fish sauce (*nước mắm*)
1 tablespoon sesame seeds
¼ teaspoon freshly ground black
   pepper
1 tablespoon Oriental sesame oil

MEAT

1 pound lean, boneless top or
   bottom beef round, in 1 chunk
   about 4 inches in diameter

ACCOMPANIMENTS FOR SERVING

Fresh Rice Papers (page 43)
Fresh mint leaves
A few sprigs coriander (Chinese
   parsley)

Nước Lèo (page 35)

 If you are using dried lemon grass, it must be soaked for 2 hours in warm water and then chopped very fine.

Slice the beef ⅛ inch thick and place the slices in a bowl.

In a mortar, pound the garlic, sugar, and shallots into a paste, then add the fish sauce, sesame seeds, black pepper, sesame oil, and lemon grass. If you are using fresh lemon grass, remove and discard the large outer leaves and ⅔ of green stalk; slice the remainder into fine crosswise slices and then chop fine. Combine with beef and marinate for 1 hour.

Preheat oven to 450 degrees. Cover the bottom and sides of a baking pan with aluminum foil. Spread the beef slices over the bottom of the pan allowing the pieces to touch and overlap. This will prevent the meat from drying. Bake for 10 minutes in the center of the oven.

To serve, let the meat cool to room temperature. Cut each rice paper in half. Put a small piece of beef on the narrow end of the paper, then a mint leaf and some coriander on top of the beef. Roll cylinder fashion. Trim the edges and arrange on a platter.

Serve with *nước lèo* as an appetizer or as a part of a party dinner.

Barbecued Beef with Lemon Grass and Noodles

Bún Thịt Bò Nướng

When Bạch invites friends to dinner, they never fail to make this noodle variation of the preceding recipe a special request — as will your guests.

Beef cooked this way can also be served with rice.

6 servings

1 pound lean, boneless top or bottom round, prepared as for Barbecued Beef Wrapped in Fresh Rice Papers (pages 92–93)

½ pound rice sticks (*bún*) or Japanese alimentary paste noodles (*somen*)

1 cup shredded cucumber

2 cups shredded lettuce

¼ cup chopped fresh mint leaves

¼ cup chopped fresh coriander (Chinese parsley)

10 Roasted Peanuts (page 46), coarsely chopped

1 fresh or dried hot red chili pepper, shredded

Whole coriander sprigs for garnish

Nước Chấm (page 34) or Nước Lèo (page 35)

While the meat is cooling to room temperature, cook the noodles according to the directions on page 44 or 45.

To serve, arrange the food in the following manner, a bowl for each diner:

Place some cucumbers and lettuce in the bottom of each bowl, then sprinkle on some of the mint and coriander. Distribute the noodles among the 6 bowls. Place the barbecued beef over the noodles. Sprinkle with more mint and parsley, plus the roasted chopped peanuts. Add a few pieces of shredded hot pepper on top and decorate with a sprig of coriander.

Serve with a bowl of *nước chấm* or *nước lèo*.

Vietnamese Roast Beef with Ginger Sauce

Bê Thui

A deservedly universal favorite among the Vietnamese, this northern specialty is never prepared at home. On different days during the week, and on most weekends, the sign "Vietnamese Roast Beef Today" is put out in front of the stores specializing in this delicacy. These stores are always owned by northerners. Each roast beef purchase is accompanied by a quantity of roasted rice powder. The consumer simply prepares the sauce and slices the roast beef.

6 servings

1 pound beef fillet
3 tablespoons Roasted Rice
    Powder (page 23)
1 scallion, both white and green
    parts, cut into 2-inch lengths
    and shredded
1 tablespoon plus ½ teaspoon
    granulated sugar

2 cloves garlic
1 fresh hot red chili pepper
3 slices fresh gingerroot
3 tablespoons *tương*
2 tablespoons water

Preheat the oven to 350 degrees. Line a baking pan with aluminum foil and place the beef fillet in it. Bake for 15 minutes, then remove from oven.

Cut the fillet into 4 chunks and then into thin 2 × 2-inch pieces. Arrange on a platter in overlapping layers and sprinkle on the powdered rice. Decorate with scallion shreds.

Put the sugar, garlic, chili pepper, and ginger into a mortar and crush with a pestle. Add the *tương* and water and mix thoroughly.

To serve, each diner helps himself to some of the meat and sprinkles some sauce over it.

Shaking Beef

Bò Lúc Lắc

The title is an exact translation from the Vietnamese, and Bạch thinks the name describes the action of the beef cubes while they are cooking. This incredibly good appetizer, spiced with garlic, is usually served as an evening snack.

Vietnamese are familiar with the use of olive oil in salad dressing. However, this reflection of the influence of French cuisine is generally too expensive to be served in restaurants and is used only at home.

6 servings

½ pound beefsteak (sirloin, fillet, porterhouse)
5 cloves garlic, chopped
1 teaspoon fish sauce (*nước mắm*)
½ teaspoon granulated sugar
½ teaspoon salt
3 teaspoons vegetable oil

1 medium onion
1 tablespoon vinegar
Sprinkling of freshly ground black pepper
1 tablespoon olive oil
2 cups watercress, with only heavy stems removed

Cut the beef into 1-inch cubes, then combine with 4 cloves of the garlic. Sprinkle on the fish sauce, sugar, ¼ teaspoon of the salt, and 2 teaspoons of the vegetable oil. Mix and allow to marinate for 30 minutes.

Slice the onion in half lengthwise and then into paper-thin slices. Marinate in the vinegar for 5 to 10 minutes, then sprinkle on the black pepper, ¼ teaspoon salt, and the olive oil. Combine the watercress with the onion marinade and arrange on a platter.

Heat the remaining teaspoon of vegetable oil in a small frying pan or wok. Add the remaining clove of garlic and stir, then add the meat. Fry quickly until seared on the outside and slightly pink in the center. Pour over the watercress and serve.

Beef Simmered with Coconut Water and Lemon Grass

Bò Kho

Very tasty and just a bit spicy is this popular combination of curry, lemon grass, and coconut water. Instead of going to a Hanoi Soup restaurant for breakfast, one goes to a breakfast restaurant that serves *bò kho* and a few other dishes. *Bò kho* is served with French bread for breakfast, as a main dish with rice, or with rice sticks (*bún*) or Japanese alimentary paste noodles (*somen*) for lunch or dinner.

6 servings

1 stalk fresh lemon grass or 1
    tablespoon dried
1¼ pounds boneless beef shank
2 teaspoons granulated sugar
1 tablespoon salt
4 cloves garlic, chopped
Dash of freshly ground black
    pepper
1 tablespoon vegetable oil
1 teaspoon tomato paste

3 bay leaves
2 cups cold water
½ teaspoon curry powder
1 large carrot, peeled and cut into
    1-inch slices
Clear water from 1 coconut (see
    page 14)
2 potatoes (about ½ pound),
    peeled and cut into 1-inch
    chunks

If you are using fresh lemon grass, remove the outer leaves and upper two-thirds of the stalk; then cut the remainder into 2-inch lengths and bruise with the back of a knife. If you are using dried, it must be soaked for 2 hours, then drained and chopped fine.

Cut the beef into cubes as for stew. Sprinkle over the meat 1 teaspoon each of sugar and salt, 1 clove of the chopped garlic, and the black pepper. Allow to marinate for 30 minutes.

Heat the oil; add the remaining garlic and fry it until it develops an aroma. Add the tomato paste, bay leaves, and lemon grass and stir for 1 minute, then add the meat and stir for a few minutes more. Add the cold water and curry powder and stir well; cover and simmer for 1½ hours.

When the simmering time is up, add the carrots, coconut water, and remaining salt and sugar and simmer for 15 minutes, covered. Add the potatoes and cook for 15 minutes longer.

Stir-Fried Beef with Green Peppers and Broccoli

Thịt Bò Xào Ớt Xanh

The Vietnamese love vegetables, and here versatile broccoli has been adopted by Bạch, in her American version of a Vietnamese stir-fried dish.

6 servings

6 ounces top beef round, in 1
  chunk (3 × 1 inches)
Sprinkling of freshly ground
  black pepper
1½ teaspoons fish sauce (*nước
  mắm*)
2 cloves garlic, minced
6 ounces broccoli florets with 1½
  inches of stem attached
1 stalk celery
1 teaspoon oyster sauce

1 teaspoon cornstarch
½ teaspoon thin soy sauce
½ cup plus 1 tablespoon water
1½ tablespoons vegetable oil
2 shallots or white part of 2
  scallions, chopped
1 large tomato, cut into 8 wedges
½ large onion, cut into 3 wedges
  and segments separated
1 green pepper, cut into 1½-inch
  squares

Slice the beef paper thin, across the grain. Sprinkle with black pepper, ½ teaspoon of the fish sauce, and half the chopped garlic. Slice broccoli through florets and stem lengthwise, into thin slices. Slice the celery stalk very thin, on the slant.

Combine the remaining 1 teaspoon fish sauce, the oyster sauce, cornstarch, soy sauce, and the ½ cup water and set aside.

Preheat a frying pan and add the oil. When the oil is hot, add the remaining garlic and the shallots. Stir for about 1 minute, then add the meat. Keep stirring for another minute; add the broccoli and the 1 tablespoon water, then stir, cover, and cook for about 3 minutes. Uncover and add the tomatoes, onion, green pepper, and celery. Stir. Add the oyster sauce mixture. Cook for 5 more minutes and serve at once, with rice and Nước Chấm (page 34) as part of a family dinner.

Stir-Fried Beef with Celery

Thịt Bò Xào Cần

6 servings

6 ounces lean beef round or flank
  steak
2 teaspoons fish sauce (*nước mắm*)
Sprinkling of freshly ground
  black pepper
1 green pepper, cut into 10
  lengthwise pieces
2 stalks celery with leaves, sliced ¼
  inch thick on the slant
1 tomato, cut into 8 wedges
1 small onion, cut into 4 wedges
1 tablespoon cornstarch
½ cup water
1 teaspoon granulated sugar
½ teaspoon vinegar
1 tablespoon vegetable oil
1 clove garlic, peeled and
  chopped

Slice the beef thin and marinate in 1 teaspoon of the fish sauce and a sprinkling of black pepper for 20 minutes. Arrange all the vegetables on a platter.

Combine the cornstarch, water, sugar, vinegar, and remaining teaspoon of fish sauce in a bowl.

Heat the oil over a high flame. Add the garlic and stir, then drop the meat in. Stir-fry for 1 minute, then, while the meat is still red, add the vegetables and the sauce immediately. Cook for about 2 minutes in all.

Serve with rice.

Beef and French-Fried Potatoes

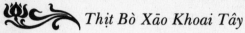 *Thịt Bò Xão Khoai Tây*

The sweet potato is native to Vietnam. Over one hundred years ago, however, the French introduced the white potato; its Vietnamese name means "Western potato." This dish is an intriguing example of a unique Vietnamese adaptation of a Western ingredient. Here the French-fried potatoes are not eaten separately, as in Western tradition. Instead, they are stir-fried in combination with the other ingredients *after* they have been fried separately — and your family will love it! Indeed, this is Bạch's mother's favorite dish.

6 servings

½ cup vegetable oil, approximately

2 large potatoes, peeled, sliced ½ inch thick, and cut into thin strips

6 ounces lean beef round, sliced paper thin

1 medium onion, cut into 8 lengthwise wedges

2 scallions, both white and green parts, cut in 2-inch lengths

1 medium tomato, cut into 8 wedges

1 green pepper, cut into 1-inch squares

1½ teaspoons cornstarch

5 tablespoons water

2 teaspoons fish sauce (*nướ́c mắm*)

2 cloves garlic, crushed and minced

Few sprigs of fresh coriander (Chinese parsley)

Sprinkling of freshly ground black pepper

Pour oil into a frying pan to a depth of ½ inch. Drop in all of the potatoes and fry until brown, then remove and set aside. (The potatoes can wait after this initial cooking for up to a few hours, until the final completion of the dish.) Drain all but 2 tablespoons of the oil from the pan.

Arrange the beef and the cut vegetables on a platter. Combine the cornstarch, water, and fish sauce.

Reheat the 2 tablespoons of oil in the pan and add the garlic. Stir, then add the onion and stir briefly, just enough to coat with oil; add the beef and stir-fry for a short time, then, while the beef is still quite red, add the scallions, tomato, and green pepper. Stir and add the cornstarch–fish sauce mixture. Add the fried potatoes, stir well to combine, and remove to a serving platter. Garnish with sprigs of coriander and sprinkle black pepper over all.

Serve with rice and Nướ́c Chấm (page 34).

Stir-Fried Beef and Cauliflower with Golden Mushrooms

Thịt Bò Xào Bông Cải Nấm Vàng

Golden mushrooms, tiny caps on long, slender stems, impart their own delicate flavor to this stir-fried dish. Cauliflower is found quite frequently in Vietnamese stir-fried dishes and provides a crisp contrast of texture and color in this beguilingly flavored dish. Golden mushrooms in cans are readily available in Oriental groceries.

6 servings

½ cup liquid from golden mushroom can
1 teaspoon cornstarch
2 teaspoons fish sauce (*nước mắm*)
½ teaspoon granulated sugar
Freshly ground black pepper
1 teaspoon oyster sauce
4 ounces beef round, sliced thin, then cut into 2 × 1-inch pieces
¼ head cauliflower (about ½ pound)

2 tablespoons vegetable oil
2 cloves garlic, peeled and chopped
1 small onion, sliced into quarters lengthwise
½ can golden mushrooms
2 sprigs fresh coriander leaves (Chinese parsley), for garnish

Combine the mushroom liquid with the cornstarch, 1 teaspoon of the fish sauce, the sugar, a sprinkling of black pepper, and the oyster sauce. Sprinkle the remaining teaspoon fish sauce and some black pepper over the meat. Separate the cauliflower into florets and then slice each one into ¼-inch lengthwise slices.

Heat the oil over a high flame and add the garlic and onion. Stir well and add the cauliflower. Cover, turn the heat down to medium, and cook for 3 minutes. Uncover and add the meat and mushrooms, stirring until there is no trace of redness in the meat. Restir the cornstarch – oyster sauce mixture and add to the pan, stirring until slightly thickened. Transfer to a platter, sprinkle Chinese parsley over the top, and serve.

NOTE

If you wish, you can also use strips of green pepper along with the cauliflower for added color and texture. If golden mushrooms are unavailable, you can substitute straw mushrooms.

Ground Beef with Lemon Grass and Shrimp Sauce

Thịt Bò Ruốc Sả

This is a superb example of a perfect blend. The strong flavor and aroma of the shrimp sauce does a remarkable disappearing act in the cooking process.

6 servings

1 stalk fresh lemon grass or 1 tablespoon dried
1½ tablespoons vegetable oil
2 shallots or white part of 2 scallions, chopped
1 clove garlic, chopped
½ pound ground beef

2 tablespoons shrimp sauce (*mắm ruốc*)
2 tablespoons raw sesame seeds
2 tablespoons granulated sugar
Sprinkling of freshly ground black pepper

If you are using fresh lemon grass, discard the outer leaves and upper two-thirds of the stalk, slice the remainder crosswise thinly and chop fine. If using dried lemon grass, it must be soaked in hot water for 2 hours, then drained and chopped fine.

Heat the oil in a frying pan or wok over a high flame. Add the combined shallots and garlic and fry for 1 minute; add the lemon grass, then stir and add the beef. Keep mixing constantly to separate the beef and to eliminate large pieces. Turn the heat down to medium and fry until the meat turns white. Add the shrimp sauce, sesame seeds, sugar, and black pepper. Keep stirring until the meat becomes quite dry. Remove from the pan and serve with rice.

NOTE

This can be stirred and dried even more. When the meat is prepared in this manner, it can be stored in a jar, kept in the refrigerator for several days, and eaten at any time, sprinkled over rice.

Pork

The versatility of pork is well demonstrated in Vietnamese cookery. Like beef, it is slaughtered and sold daily.

Although Vietnamese pork has a fine reputation for quality in general, it is the pork in Hue, the Center, that is exceptional in quality. The pigs are smaller than usual, the meat is tender and less fatty, and the skin is thinner. They are fed banana tree trunk and rice, which accounts for their superb flavor.

Pork is far and away the most popular meat in Vietnam, not only for its versatility, but for its low price. Until recently, pork lard was widely used in cooking, but vegetable oils are now used for the most part in its place.

Barbecued Pork with Rice Noodles

 *Bún Thịt Nướng*

Although the title would suggest barbecuing as the method of preparation, for the convenience of Westerners we suggest baking. Credit for this toothsome combination of pork butt and roasted peanuts goes to the North, although it is found everywhere.

6 servings

½ pound rice sticks (*bún*) or 2½ packets of Japanese alimentary paste noodles (*somen*)
3 shallots or white part of 3 scallions
2 cloves garlic
1 tablespoon granulated sugar
1½ tablespoons fish sauce (*nước mắm*)
⅛ teaspoon freshly ground black pepper
¼ teaspoon MSG (optional)

1 pound pork butt, sliced paper thin against the grain
Double recipe of Nước Chấm (page 34)
3 tablespoons Roasted Peanuts (page 46), coarsely chopped
Carrot and Sweet Radish in Vinegar (page 39)
2 scallions, green part only, thinly sliced
Basic Vegetable Platter (pages 37–38)

Prepare the rice sticks according to the directions on page 44.

Combine the shallots, garlic, and sugar in a mortar and pound to a paste. Add the fish sauce, black pepper, and optional MSG.

Marinate the meat in the shallot-garlic mixture for 1 hour.

Preheat the oven to 450 degrees. Line a baking pan with aluminum foil. Arrange the pork on the foil in overlapping slices. (It's best not to separate the pieces, as this will cause them to dry while cooking.) Bake for 20 minutes on one side; then turn the pieces over and bake for an additional 20 minutes. Remove from the oven.

To serve, place the pork in individual bowls, preferably shallow ones. Sprinkle with *nước chấm*, enough to cover the pork almost completely. Sprinkle with the roasted peanuts, then add radish and carrot flowers to cover the meat. Sprinkle with thinly sliced scallion greens.

Each person is given another bowl containing a small amount of noodles. From the large vegetable platter, he then takes a little of each vegetable.

and puts them over the noodles. The diner transfers small amounts of the contents of the pork bowl into the noodle bowl and eats from the noodle bowl.

NOTE

The pork can be cooked a few hours ahead, wrapped in foil, and reheated.

Pork Cooked with Coconut Water

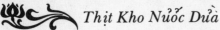 *Thịt Kho Nước Dừa*

Bạch had never eaten this dish in her own home. When she got married her husband took her to a restaurant, where she was able to analyze the recipe and reproduce it at home. Because of her sensitive palate, she has always been able to do this.

This is a very well-known family dish in South Vietnam, usually served in restaurants for lunch or dinner with rice.

6 servings

1½ pounds boneless fresh ham or porkshoulder, with rind attached
2½ cups water, more if necessary
Clear water from 1 coconut
7 tablespoons fish sauce (*nước mắm*)

7 teaspoons granulated sugar
Sprinkling of freshly ground black pepper
2 tablespoons Caramelized Sugar (page 47)

Cut meat into strips 1 inch thick and about 2 inches in length. (Some pieces of the pork will have the rind attached. Do not discard this rind, as it is an important ingredient of the recipe.)

Bring the water to a boil. Drop the meat in and return to the boil; continue to boil, uncovered, for 15 minutes. After the initial boiling period, cover the pot and lower the heat to a simmer. When the meat has started to cook at a simmer, crack open a fresh coconut (see page 14), and pour the coconut water into the pot. Continue cooking the meat at a simmer for another hour, or until the meat is very tender.

When the meat is sufficiently tender, uncover the pot. If at this point the water level has decreased substantially, and is not at about the same level or a little below the level of the meat in the pot, add enough water to bring it up to that point. Then add the fish sauce, granulated sugar, sprinkling of black pepper, and caramelized sugar to the liquid and simmer for another 15 minutes. Serve with rice and Sour Bean Sprouts (page 40).

Fried Pork with Tomato Sauce

Heo Ram Sốt Cà

Bạch calls this her "lazy" dish. When she's tired, she cooks this, and with some rice it's a complete family dinner.

6 servings

1 tablespoon vegetable oil
1¼ pounds pork chops, each 1
  inch thick
3 tablespoons fish sauce (nước
  mắm)

3 tablespoons thin soy sauce
¾ cup water
5 tablespooons granulated sugar
1 tablespoon tomato paste
2 cloves garlic, chopped

Heat the oil in a frying pan over a medium flame. Put the pork chops into the pan and cover. Brown; turn and brown the other side, still covered. After about 30 minutes, when the pork is completely browned, prepare the sauce by combining the fish sauce, soy sauce, water, sugar, and tomato paste in a bowl.

Push the chops to one side of the pan and add the chopped garlic. Stir, then add the combined sauce mixture. Bring to a boil, then arrange the pork chops over the sauce. Simmer, uncovered, for 10 minutes, or until the liquid thickens.

Remove the chops from the pan and slice across the grain into strips ¼ inch thick. Each person is given a platter of rice, some pork strips are placed on top, and the remaining sauce is poured over.

Pork Simmered with Five Spice Powder
Thịt Thủng

This is one of Bạch's husband's favorites, a dish that his mother cooked. Although both Bạch's and Nhon's mothers were from the Center, they both had different styles of cooking. Shortly after Bạch was married, she spent time at the home of her mother-in-law to observe and learn to cook many of her husband's favorites.

In this recipe we give you the option of using pork shoulder or pork butt. The shoulder usually has the rind or skin attached, and although we find it delicious, some people do not wish to use the fat that is attached to the meat. In that case, pork butt is just as good. The use of five spice powder lends a very special flavor to this dish.

6 servings

2 cloves garlic
2 shallots or white part of 2
  scallions
1½ tablespoons granulated sugar
1 tablespoon fish sauce (nước
  mắm)
6 tablespoons water

2 tablespoons light soy sauce
⅜ teaspoon five spice powder
Sprinkling of freshly ground
  black pepper
1 tablespoon vegetable oil
½ pound pork shoulder with
  rind, or pork butt

In a mortar, mash the garlic, shallots, and sugar; add the fish sauce, water, soy sauce, five spice powder, and black pepper.

Heat the vegetable oil in a small saucepan over a high flame. Drop the pork into the pot to brown. Keep covered, uncovering only to turn the meat from time to time. After the meat is well browned, add the sauce mixture. Cover and turn the flame down to medium.

After 15 minutes, turn the pork in the sauce to color the meat. Continue cooking for another 15 minutes, covered, uncovering periodically to check the progress of the cooking. When you see only small bubbles and about 5 tablespoons of liquid, the cooking is completed.

Remove the meat and allow to cool slightly, then slice, arrange on a platter and pour the remaining sauce over. Serve with rice and Sour Bean Sprouts (page 40).

Steamed Pork

Thịt Chủng

Bạch invented this recipe for her children. When she makes a large dinner and knows that the children, like children of all lands, won't like everything, she is always certain that they will devour this.

4 servings

1 ounce cellophane noodles
4 ounces ground beef
½ pound ground pork
1 medium onion, chopped
2 eggs
2 shallots or white part of 2
  scallions, chopped

1 clove garlic, chopped
Sprinkling of freshly ground
  black pepper
2 teaspoons fish sauce (*nước mắm*)

Soak the cellophane noodles in warm water for 20 minutes, then drain and chop fine. Combine the beef and ground pork. Add the cellophane noodles and the remaining ingredients and mix well with your hands. Transfer the mixture to a bowl, then place the bowl in a pot of water reaching halfway up the bowl. Bring to boil; turn the heat down to medium and cover the pot (but not the bowl, as you want the wet steam to circulate freely and cook the food). Steam for 40 minutes.

NOTE

This can be kept warm in the pot until serving time, keeping the heat as low as possible. Serve with rice.

Pork Hock Simmered with Lemon Grass
Giò Heo Hon

The sophisticated combination of lemon grass, roasted peanuts, and curry powder with chewy pork hocks is typical of the true Center dish. Serve with rice. (Bach's father-in-law eats this for breakfast with glutinous rice.)

4 servings

1 stalk fresh lemon grass or 1 tablespoon dried
3 cups water
2 pork hocks (about 1½ pounds), cut into slices 1 inch thick
½ cup Roasted Peanuts (page 46), halved

¾ teaspoon curry powder
1 tablespoon salt
2 tablespoons granulated sugar
Sprinkling of freshly ground pepper

If you are using fresh lemon grass, simply discard the outer leaves and upper two-thirds of the stalk. If you are using dried, it must be soaked in warm water for 2 hours, then drained.

Bring the 3 cups of water to a boil. Drop in the pork hocks and lemon grass. Remove the scum that forms as soon as it returns to the boil, then cover and simmer for 1½ hours.

After the pork hocks have simmered for 1½ hours, add the roasted peanuts, curry powder, salt, sugar, and black pepper. Mix well and continue to simmer for another 30 minutes, or until there is about 1 cup of liquid left in the pot. Serve with rice or glutinous rice.

Tomatoes Stuffed with Ground Pork
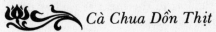 *Cà Chua Dồn Thịt*

Fine Vietnamese cooks are as creative as fine cooks in other cultures. Although she had many servants, Madame Sưởng, Bạch's mother, always cooked or closely supervised all cooking in her kitchen. This is one of the many recipes she developed. The full aroma and rich flavor of the sauce, resulting from the unusual blend of garlic, fish sauce, and thin soy sauce, will make this a family favorite.

4 servings

STUFFED TOMATOES

4 medium, not-too-ripe tomatoes
2 cloves garlic, finely chopped
¼ small onion, finely chopped
2 shallots or white part of 2
   scallions, chopped
6 ounces ground pork

½ teaspoon granulated sugar
2 teaspoons fish sauce (*nước mắm*)
Sprinkling of freshly ground
   black pepper
¼ cup vegetable oil

SAUCE

¼ cup water
1 tablespoon fish sauce (*nước mắm*)
1 tablespoon granulated sugar
1 tablespoon thin soy sauce

1 teaspoon vegetable oil
1 clove garlic, peeled and chopped
1½ teaspoons tomato paste

GARNISH

Sprigs of fresh coriander
   (Chinese parsley)

 Cut the tops off the tomatoes and remove the pulp with a spoon. Discard the tops and the pulp.

Add the chopped garlic, onion, and shallots to the meat as well as the sugar, fish sauce, and pepper. Mix well with your hands.

Dry the insides of the tomatoes with a paper towel. (It is important that they be dry to prevent the mixture from falling out.) Stuff the tomatoes with the meat, pressing it in firmly.

Heat the oil in a frying pan or a wok. Add the tomatoes, meat side down. Cover, turn the heat to medium, and cook for 5 minutes. Turn the tomatoes, meat side up, and cook covered for another 5 minutes. While the tomatoes are cooking, prepare the sauce.

Combine the water, fish sauce, sugar, and soy sauce in a bowl.

Heat the oil over a high flame with the garlic. Add the tomato paste and stir for about 1 minute, then add the combined liquids. Stir for about 2 minutes at a strong boil and pour over the tomatoes.

Decorate the platter with sprigs of coriander and serve with rice.

NOTE

This dish can also be served without the sauce.

Stuffed Bean Curd
Tàu Hủ Nhồi Thịt

The same superb tomato sauce from the recipe for Tomatoes Stuffed with Ground Pork (pages 111–12) graces another and quite different dish developed by Madame Sương.

6 servings

4 squares bean curd
4 ounces ground pork
2 shallots or white part of 2
   scallions
Sprinkling of freshly ground
   black pepper

1 teaspoon fish sauce (*nước mắm*)
½ teaspoon granulated sugar
¼ cup vegetable oil
Tomato sauce, prepared as for
   Tomatoes Stuffed with Ground
   Pork (pages 111–12)

Cut each bean curd square in half to make 2 thin slices. Combine the remaining ingredients except for the oil and tomato sauce. Spread one-fourth of the mixture over each slice of the bean curd and place another slice on top, to form a "sandwich." Repeat this procedure with the remaining bean curd.

Heat the oil in a frying pan over a high flame. Place the bean curd "sandwiches" into the oil, cover the pan, and turn the heat down to medium. Uncover the pan from time to time, and turn the bean curd to brown both sides. When they are completely browned, remove from pan and cut each sandwich into 9 one-inch squares. Reheat the tomato sauce and pour over the bean curd. Serve with rice.

Pork and Shrimp Simmered with Fish Sauce

Tôm Thịt Kho Rim

4 servings

½ pound lean fresh ham or pork loin, in 1 chunk

4 ounces raw shrimp

3 tablespoons fish sauce (*nước mắm*)

2 tablespoons plus 1 teaspoon granulated sugar

⅛ teaspoon freshly ground black pepper

2 teaspoons Caramelized Sugar (page 47)

1 tablespoon vegetable oil

2 shallots or white part of 2 scallions, finely chopped

Slice the pork ½ inch thick, then cut into pieces ½ inch wide and 2 inches in length. Shell and devein the shrimp, keeping on the tail section of the shell to make the shrimp attractive in appearance.

Put the pork into a small saucepan; pour over the fish sauce, sugar, pepper, and caramelized sugar. Turn the heat to high, stirring for about 3 minutes, or until the liquid comes to a boil. Reduce the heat to medium, cover, and cook for 7 minutes.

Halfway through the meat's cooking time, heat the oil in a small frying pan over high heat. Drop in the shallots and stir, then add the shrimp, stir for 3 minutes, and transfer to the saucepan containing the meat. Stir the meat and shrimp together, then cook, covered, for 10 minutes, or until there are about 8 tablespoons of liquid left in the saucepan. Serve with rice.

Bean Sprouts Fried with Shrimp and Pork
Giá Xào Tôm Thịt

4 servings

2 ounces fresh ham, pork loin, or
  pork butt, shredded
2 teaspoons fish sauce (*nước mắm*)
Freshly ground black pepper
2 ounces small raw shrimp,
  unshelled, or large raw shrimp,
  shelled, deveined, and sliced

1 tablespoon vegetable oil
2 shallots or white part of 2
  scallions, finely chopped
½ pound fresh bean sprouts
1 sprig fresh coriander (Chinese
  parsley)

Marinate the pork for 10 minutes in 1 teaspoon of the fish sauce and a sprinkling of black pepper. Marinate the shrimp in the same way.

Heat the oil over a high flame and add the shallots; stir for 1 minute and add the meat. Continue to stir for 7 to 10 minutes; add the shrimp and stir for another 3 minutes, then add the bean sprouts and continue to stir for 2 minutes more. Remove from the heat and transfer to a serving platter. Sprinkle some additional black pepper over the food and garnish with a sprig of coriander. Serve with rice.

Three-Meat Vegetable Dish

Xāo Thập Cẩm

Xāo thập cẩm means "many varieties of meat and vegetables," and that is exactly what we have here. If you don't have every one of the ingredients, just omit from the recipe.

This is a good party dish.

6 servings

2 ounces boneless chicken breast
  or thigh, in thin strips
2 ounces lean pork, in thin strips
2 ounces beef (sirloin, flank steak,
  round), in thin strips
1 tablespoon plus 1 teaspoon fish
  sauce (*nước mắm*)
5 dried Chinese mushrooms
1 teaspoon cornstarch
½ cup cold water
1 teaspoon oyster sauce
1 tablespoon vegetable oil
1 shallot or white part of 1
  scallion, sliced

2 cloves garlic, minced
1 medium onion, thinly sliced
1 cup sliced bamboo shoots
1 carrot, peeled and sliced
  lengthwise with a carrot peeler,
  in strips as wide as possible
¼ cup raw cashew nuts
2 ounces snow peas, strings
  removed
10 quail eggs (optional)
½ green pepper, cut into thin
  strips

Place the chicken, pork, and beef on separate platters and sprinkle each with 1 teaspoon fish sauce. Soak the mushrooms in warm water for 30 minutes, then squeeze dry and cut each one into 4 sections. Combine the cornstarch, water, remaining fish sauce, and oyster sauce; set aside.

Heat the oil in a large frying pan and add shallot and garlic. Stir for 1 minute then add the chicken and pork; stir for 2 minutes. Add the beef, onion, mushrooms, bamboo shoots, and carrot. Stir briefly to combine all the ingredients, then cover, turning the heat down to medium; keep covered for 3 minutes. Uncover and add the cashews, snow peas, quail eggs, and green pepper. Stir for 3 minutes more. Add the cornstarch mixture after restirring and stir until all the ingredients are covered with sauce.

NOTE

Quail eggs can be purchased in Oriental grocery stores.

Cotton Meat
Thịt Chà Bông

A dish especially favored in the North, its name comes from its appearance after having been cooked dry.

It is often served for breakfast in rice soup or with a bowl of rice for dinner, and is delightful in a sandwich of French bread with cucumbers, coriander (Chinese parsley), pickled carrots, or any one of those and a scallion, sprinkled with thin soy sauce or Maggi sauce.

4 servings

1 pound lean, boneless pork loin, in 1 chunk

5 tablespoons fish sauce (*nước mắm*)

Slice the meat ¾ inch thick and then into pieces 3 inches wide. Place in a small saucepan, along with the fish sauce. Cover and simmer for 10 minutes, or until all the liquid has evaporated. Turn the meat after the first 5 minutes to make certain it is well cooked.

When cooked, put a few pieces at a time into a mortar and pound with a pestle until completely crushed and stringy. (If you have a large mortar, you can do about 3 pieces at a time. It cannot be done in a food processor, as the meat must remain stringy.) As each piece of meat is crushed, it should be pulled apart with the fingers.

After all the meat is shredded, transfer it to a dry frying pan over low heat, and with a wooden spoon keep pressing it down and spreading it about. Continue doing this until the meat is completely dry. When you hear no sizzling sound coming from the frying pan, you know that the meat is ready.

Serve as suggested above.

NOTE

Cotton Meat will keep in a refrigerated jar for several weeks.

Poultry and Eggs

Chicken and duck are highly prized in Vietnam for their versatility. They are served only on special occasions because of their high price. Vietnamese chickens are not kept to fatten in cages, as in the United States, but run free. Consequently, they are not tender, but the Vietnamese prefer them to the American chicken. The white breast meat is never dry — due, some say, to their being fed raw rice. In any case, every part of the chicken is used.

Glutinous Rice-Stuffed Boneless Whole Chicken

Gā Rút Xương Nhối Nếp

8 servings

2 cups sweet or glutinous rice
1 cup coconut milk, fresh or canned
1¼ cups chicken broth, fresh or canned
1 chicken (3½ pounds)
1½ teaspoons salt
Freshly ground black pepper

2 cloves garlic, chopped
½ cup straw mushrooms
½ teaspoon granulated sugar
1½ cups plus 2 teaspoons vegetable oil
1 shallot, chopped
Juice of ½ lemon

Cook sweet or glutinous rice in the cocount milk and broth, following the directions on page 42. Allow the rice to cool for 1 hour.

Bone the chicken completely (see page 122); remove the leg meat from the carcass and set aside. (The leg portion, with the skin still intact, will be stuffed with sweet or glutinous rice, thus retaining the original shape of the chicken.)

Spread the chicken open and sprinkle over it 1 teaspoon of the salt, ¼ teaspoon black pepper, and half the chopped garlic. Dice the reserved leg meat and straw mushrooms small. Combine the diced chicken and mushrooms with the ½ teaspoon salt, the sugar, and a sprinkling of black pepper.

Heat the 2 teaspoons of oil in a frying pan. Fry the chopped shallot and remaining garlic until lightly browned, then add the chicken-mushroom mixture and stir-fry over high heat for about 5 minutes, or until the chicken is completely cooked.

Combine the cooled rice with the chicken-mushroom mixture and spread the rice filling on the inside of the boned chicken, forcing it into the thigh cavities, and mold to resemble the thighs. After the chicken has been completely stuffed, reshape into its original form as closely as possible and sew closed with a needle and white thread.

Rub the juice of ½ lemon over the entire surface of the skin. Heat the 1½ cups of oil in a large frying pan over a high flame. Place the chicken into the oil. Reduce heat to medium and cook until chicken is well browned on all sides. Remove from pan and cut into horizontal slices.

Serve warm with Nước Chấm (page 34) as a main dish; for parties, serve cool.

Chicken Steamed with Ham and Chinese Cabbage

Gà Chửng Jambon

The French influence is apparent in the title, although the recipe is totally Vietnamese in concept.

The pink dome of ham concealing the chicken, encircled by the pale green cabbage, is a lovely centerpiece for an elegant party or a festive family dinner.

Serve hot, with or without rice.

4 servings

5 slices boiled ham	¾ teaspoon salt
2 stalks *bok choy*	¼ teaspoon freshly ground black
5 chicken thighs	pepper
½ onion, chopped	1½ teaspoons granulated sugar
1 clove garlic, chopped	2 teaspoons cornstarch
2 shallots, chopped	½ teaspoon black soy sauce
1 tablespoon fish sauce (*nước mắm*)	1 cup chicken stock, canned or fresh

Cut each slice of ham into 4 sections. Line a 3-cup bowl with the ham, in overlapping layers. Cut the *bok choy* into 2-inch chunks. Slice through the white stalks of the *bok choy* to make them thinner.

Remove the chicken from the thighs in strips 1 inch wide and the full length of the thighs. Combine the chicken, onion, garlic, and shallots with 1 teaspoon of the fish sauce, ¼ of the teaspoon salt, the black pepper, and ½ teaspoon of the sugar, mixing well with hands.

Pour the chicken mixture into the ham-lined bowl and pat down to firm. Set the bowl into a pot of boiling water, reaching halfway up the side of bowl. Cover and steam the chicken mixture for 35 minutes. Then put the *bok choy* on top of the bowl and steam for another 5 minutes.

While the chicken and *bok choy* are steaming, combine the cornstarch, remaining 2 teaspoons fish sauce, ½ teaspoon salt, 1 teaspoon sugar, soy sauce, and stock. Boil until thickened.

Uncover the steamer. Remove the cabbage and spread it over a round platter. Then turn the contents of the bowl over the cabbage, keeping the dome shape of the bowl. Pour the sauce on top and serve.

Vietnamese Boneless Stuffed Chicken

 *Gà Rút Xửơng Nhồi*

Similar in appearance but not in taste to the French *galantine*, this delicacy is sold in Vietnamese markets in the same way that cold cuts are sold in other countries. It can also be served as an appetizer with *nửớc chấm*, and it will keep for a week if refrigerated.

8 servings

3 chicken legs with thighs plus 1 whole chicken (about 3 pounds)
3 cloves garlic, chopped
1 small onion, chopped
2 shallots or white part of 2 scallions, chopped
1½ teaspoons salt

1½ teaspoons fish sauce (*nửớc mắm*)
½ teaspoon granulated sugar
⅛ teaspoon black pepper
Lettuce, tomatoes, and radishes for garnish

Remove the bones from the legs and thighs and cut the meat into 1-inch cubes. In a bowl combine the garlic, onion, shallots, ½ teaspoon salt, fish sauce, sugar, and ⅛ teaspoon black pepper. Add the chicken cubes, mix well, and set aside to marinate. Then bone the chicken as follows:

Work from the tail end toward the neck end, with the breast side up. Using a sharp knife, carefully separate the meat from the breastbone and ribs, ending about three-quarters of the way up. With the neck side down (a sort of standing-on-head position), hold the chicken in a standing position and scrape meat from the bones. Remove the wings and set aside for some other use. Cut around the end of the drumstick to separate the meat from the bones. Rotate the knife around the carcass, separating the skeleton from the meat and thigh bones. Grasp the thigh with one hand, holding the chicken securely. With the other hand, twist the drumstick bone, using some force, to separate the drumstick from the thigh. Repeat this with the other drumstick. Withdraw and discard the skeleton.

Now bone the legs and thighs. Remove the thigh meat by scraping against the bone with your knife. Cut through the joint where the thigh bone is connected to the drumstick. Remove the thigh bone and continue scraping against the drumstick until you have separated the meat from the bone; withdraw this bone. Push the attached drumstick meat inside the chicken to close up chicken at leg joints.

Sew the neck opening and the places where the wings were attached with white thread, closing that entire end. Lay the chicken flat and rub the 1 teaspoon of salt and a dash of black pepper over the inside of the chicken.

Put the marinated chicken cubes inside the boned chicken. Draw chicken closed and sew it; then tie with string as you would tie a roast. Steam for 60 minutes directly on the upper insert of a tightly closed steamer (see Techniques, page 30).

Remove from the steamer and allow the chicken to cool, preferably overnight. Slice and arrange attractively on a platter of lettuce and tomatoes, surrounded by radish roses.

Serve with French bread or rice as an appetizer with Nước Chấm (page 34) and the above lettuce, tomato, and radish platter.

Vietnamese Curry

 *Cari*

This is a real Vietnamese curry. Although adapted from the Indian, which is always made with white potatoes, the Vietnamese version has the option of using white or sweet potatoes, the latter being greatly favored by the Vietnamese. The Indian influence is greatest in the South, where curried dishes are more popular than elsewhere in Vietnam.

This is usually served with noodles as a party dish. When it is part of a family meal, it is eaten with rice. Bach serves this to her children for breakfast, when it is served with French bread — another influence on the cuisine of Vietnam.

8 servings

1 stalk fresh lemon grass or 1
   tablespoon dried
3½ teaspoons curry powder
Sprinkling of freshly ground
   black pepper
1 teaspoon granulated sugar
4 teaspoons salt
1 chicken (3 pounds), cut into 10
   pieces (each breast cut into
   fours)
7 tablespoons vegetable oil
3 sweet potatoes or 3 white
   potatoes, peeled and cut into
   2-inch cubes

4 cloves garlic, chopped
3 bay leaves
1 large onion, cut into wedges and
   sections separated
2 cups water
1 carrot, cut into 2-inch slices
2 cups coconut milk, fresh (see
   page 48) or canned
1 cup milk or water (if you use
   canned coconut milk, you must
   use water)

If you are using fresh lemon grass, simply remove the outer leaves and upper two-thirds of the stalks, then cut the remainder into 2-inch lengths. If you are using dried, it must be soaked in warm water for 2 hours, then drained and chopped fine.

Combine the curry powder, black pepper, sugar, and salt and marinate the chicken in the mixture for at least 1 hour. Heat the oil and fry the potatoes over high heat until brown. (It is not necessary to completely cook potatoes at this point, only to brown them.) When well browned, remove from the pan and set aside until ready to cook the curry. Pour off most of the oil from the pan, leaving 2 tablespoons for cooking the chicken.

Heat 2 tablespoons oil over a high flame. Fry the garlic for a few seconds, then add the bay leaves, onion, and lemon grass; stir briefly and add the marinated chicken, stirring long enough to sear the meat slightly. Add the 2 cups of water and the carrot, then cover and bring to a boil. Turn the heat down and simmer for 5 minutes; uncover and stir, then cook, covered, for another 10 minutes. Remove the cover and add the prefried potatoes, the coconut milk, and the milk. Cover again and simmer for another 15 minutes. Serve with rice, rice sticks (page 44), or Japanese alimentary paste noodles (page 45).

Simmered Chicken with Ginger

Thịt Gà Kho Gừng

Nicely spiced with ginger, this Center dish is ideal for cooking ahead.

4 servings

4 chicken thighs
1 small piece fresh gingerroot,
 shredded
1 tablespoon plus 1 teaspoon
 granulated sugar
5 tablespoons fish sauce (*nước mắm*)

Sprinkling of freshly ground
 black pepper
1 teaspoon vegetable oil
1 clove garlic, chopped
2 tablespoons Caramelized Sugar
 (page 47)

Bone the chicken, then cut into 1-inch squares. Put in a bowl and sprinkle with the ginger, sugar, fish sauce, and black pepper.

Heat the oil in a small saucepan over a high flame. Fry the garlic. Add the chicken mixture and stir well. Cover, turn the heat down to medium, and cook for 10 minutes. Add the caramelized sugar and continue to cook, covered, for another 10 minutes, or until there are about 4 to 5 tablespoons of liquid left in the pan, visible in the form of bubbles. At this point, the chicken should be stirred well and removed from the heat. It can be reheated at serving time.

NOTE

This dish can be prepared several days ahead. Fish sauce is an excellent preservative.

Jellied Chicken

Thịt Gà Đông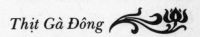

As part of a meal, this excellent northern dish is usually served with Pickled Mustard Greens (page 39) and rice; it is also served separately as an appetizer with apéritifs.

6 to 8 servings

1 tablespoon tree ears
10 strands agar-agar
3 cups water
2 chicken legs with thighs
Pork skin (a piece about the size of a hand)
2 shallots or white part of 2 scallions, chopped

2½ tablespoons fish sauce (*nước mắm*)
⅛ teaspoon freshly ground black pepper
Pinch of MSG (optional)

Soak the tree ears for 15 minutes, then drain and chop fine. Soak the agar-agar in cold water for 5 to 10 minutes; drain before using.

Bring the 3 cups of water to a boil and drop in the chicken legs and pork skin. Cook, uncovered, for 20 minutes over medium heat, then remove chicken and the pork skin from the broth. Reserve the broth in the pot.

Shred the pork skin with a sharp knife and cut the chicken into strips; cut each strip crosswise into 3 pieces. Combine in a bowl the shallots, chicken and pork, tree ears, fish sauce, black pepper, and MSG; set aside.

Return the broth to a boil. Remove the agar-agar from its bowl of water and drop into the boiling broth. After it has boiled for 5 minutes, drop in the reserved chicken–pork skin mixture. Cook, covered, at medium heat, for 15 minutes more, stirring frequently.

Pour into a 9-inch pie plate. Cool, then chill in the refrigerator for several hours, until the gelatin mixture is firm. (This becomes jellied very quickly because of the pork skin and agar-agar.) Cut into 1-inch cubes before serving as directed above.

Shredded Chicken with Small Mint Leaves
Gà Xé Phay

Well known both in the North and in the Center, this dish is served before the meal, as an appetizer, or as part of the meal.

6 servings

2 chicken legs with thighs
3 cups water
½ onion
White vinegar
⅓ cup small mint leaves (*rau răm*),
 if possible, or common mint
 leaves

¼ teaspoon salt
⅛ teaspoon freshly ground black
 pepper

Boil the chicken legs in 3 cups of water for 20 minutes, then remove from the pot and discard the broth or save it for some other use. Remove the chicken from the bones and shred.

While the chicken is cooking, slice the onion into paper-thin rings. Place in a bowl and cover with white vinegar for 10 to 15 minutes. Remove the mint leaves from the stems and chop fine.

Place the chicken in a bowl and add to it the chopped mint, salt, and pepper; mix well with your hands, continuing to mix until the salt is completely dissolved.

Remove the onions from the vinegar and rinse quickly in cold water. Add to the chicken-mint mixture, mix again, and serve.

NOTE

The varieties of mint leaves (in this case, rau răm) often used are difficult to obtain here, so we use the common mint from our gardens.

Fried Chicken with Lemon Grass and Red Pepper

Gà Xaò Sả Ớt

Some like it hot. This tasty and spicy-hot main dish will please them no end!

6 servings

1 stalk fresh lemon grass or 1 tablespoon dried
4 chicken thighs or legs
2 tablespoons fish sauce (*nước mắm*)
2 teaspoons granulated sugar
Sprinkling of freshly ground black pepper

3 cloves garlic, finely chopped
1 tablespoon vegetable oil
¼ teaspoon cayenne pepper
1 teaspoon Caramelized Sugar (page 47)

If you are using fresh lemon grass, simply discard the outer leaves and the upper two-thirds of the stalk, then chop fine. If you are using dried, it must be soaked in hot water for 2 hours, then drained and chopped fine.

Bone the chicken and cut into 1-inch cubes.

Combine 1 tablespoon of the fish sauce, the granulated sugar, black pepper, 2 cloves of the garlic, and the lemon grass. Sprinkle over the chicken cubes and let marinate for 30 minutes.

Heat the oil over a high flame and add the remaining chopped garlic, then stir and add the chicken; continue mixing for 5 minutes. Turn the heat down to medium; add the remaining tablespoon of fish sauce, the cayenne pepper, and caramelized sugar. Cook, stirring for an additional 5 minutes.

Serve with rice.

NOTE

This dish can be cooked several hours ahead and reheated.

Fried Chicken with Broccoli

Gà Xaò Broccoli

Chicken, when coated with cornstarch and deep fried, takes on a crunchiness, and when combined with the other vegetables has a very special flavor.

6 servings

CHICKEN AND VEGETABLES

2 stalks broccoli
1 small onion, cut into 4 wedges
1 tomato, cut into 8 wedges
2 scallions, both green and white part, cut into 2-inch sections
2 cloves garlic, chopped
2 chicken thighs

Sprinkling of freshly ground black pepper
1 teaspoon fish sauce (nướć mắm)
3 tablespoons cornstarch
½ cup plus 1 tablespoon vegetable oil
¼ cup water

SAUCE

½ cup water
2 teaspoons cornstarch
1 teaspoon fish sauce (nướć mắm)

½ teaspoon granulated sugar
1 teaspoon oyster sauce

Separate the broccoli florets from stalks, then slice the florets ½ inch thick. Peel the stalks; cut crosswise into 1-inch sections and then into lengthwise slices. Arrange the broccoli with the other vegetables in separate mounds on a platter. Combine the sauce ingredients in a bowl.

Bone the chicken and cut the meat into 1-inch cubes. Sprinkle with the black pepper and fish sauce, then coat with the 3 tablespoons of cornstarch.

Heat the ½ cup oil in a wok or small saucepan to 375 degrees. Deep-fry the chicken, half at a time, until brown and crisp. Remove and drain on paper towels, then transfer to a platter.

In a wok or frying pan, heat the 1 tablespoon oil over high heat. Add the garlic and stir, then add the onion; again, stir briefly, then add the scallions. After these vegetables are well combined, add the broccoli and stir for about 1 minute; add the water, reduce the heat to medium and cover for 3 minutes. Uncover the pan, then add the tomato; stir and add the sauce mixture, stirring until slightly thickened.

Pour the sauce over the chicken and serve with rice.

Fried Chicken with Vinegar and Lemon Grass

Thịt Gà Xaò Dấm Gủng Sả

The answer to a cook's prayer, the vinegar-spiked, mouth-filling flavor and sultry aroma of this dish guarantee love at first taste. Making a good thing even better, it is a fast and easy-to-prepare main dish.

4 servings

1 stalk fresh lemon grass or 1 tablespoon dried
2 tablespoons peeled, shredded fresh gingerroot
2 tablespoons vinegar
3 chicken thighs
2 tablespoons fish sauce (*nước mắm*)
Sprinkling of freshly ground black pepper

1 teaspoon cornstarch
6 tablespoons water
½ teaspoon sugar
1 tablespoon vegetable oil
3 cloves garlic, chopped
1 onion, cut into 8 wedges
1 scallion, green part only, cut into 4 pieces

If you are using fresh lemon grass, simply discard the outer leaves and upper two-thirds of the stalks; slice the remainder paper thin. If you are using dried, it must be soaked in warm water for 2 hours, then drained and chopped fine.

Cover the ginger with the 2 tablespoons vinegar and set aside.

Bone the chicken and cut into bite-size pieces. Season the chicken with 1 tablespoon of the fish sauce and sprinkle with black pepper. Add the lemon grass and mix well.

Make a paste of cornstarch, water, remaining fish sauce, and the sugar; set aside.

Heat the oil and fry the garlic; add the onion and stir briefly, then add the chicken and scallion. Fry, stirring constantly, for about 5 minutes, then cover and cook over medium heat for another 5 minutes. Uncover and add the ginger and vinegar and the cornstarch mixture; stir well. Cover again and cook for an additional 5 minutes.

Serve with rice.

Laqué Duck

Vịt Quay

This adaption from Chinese cuisine is served in restaurants throughout Vietnam. Inviting in appearance and irresistible in taste, it will vanish in a trice.

6 to 8 servings

4 teaspoons achiote (annatto seeds) or a few drops of red food coloring
¼ cup hot water
5 scallions, both white and green parts
¼ cup black soy sauce
¼ cup dark corn syrup
¼ teaspoon five spice powder
Sprinkling of freshly ground black pepper

3 tablespoons granulated sugar
Dash of MSG (optional)
1 duck (4 to 4½ pounds)
3 sprigs coriander (Chinese parsley), cut into fours
½ package dried rice noodles, the thinnest available (*bánh hỏi*)
2 tablespoons vegetable oil
Basic Vegetable Platter (pages 37–38)
Nước Chấm (page 34)

Break the achiote seeds, if using, in a mortar with a pestle or in a food processor. Soak in the hot water for 1 hour, then strain the liquid and discard the seeds.

Cut 4 of the scallions into 4 pieces crosswise; chop the remaining scallion and set aside.

Combine the colored water, soy sauce, corn syrup, five spice powder, black pepper, sugar, and MSG. Pour 3 tablespoons of this marinade inside the duck, together with the quartered scallions and coriander. Close all the openings with lacing pins, then place the duck in a bowl, pour the remaining marinade over, and allow to marinate for at least 2 hours (or as long as overnight in the refrigerator).

Preheat oven to 350 degrees. Place the duck on a rack in a roasting pan, placing the pan on the middle rack of the oven. Roast for 45 minutes, then reduce the heat to 300 degrees, turn the duck over, and roast for 45 minutes longer. Use the marinade remaining in the bowl and paint the duck every 15 minutes while roasting, until all the marinade has been used.

While the duck is roasting, bring 2 quarts of water to a boil. Drop in the noodles and boil for 1 minute. Drain in a colander and rinse under cold run-

ning water, then allow the noodles to dry for 1 hour. While the noodles are drying, fry the reserved chopped scallions in the 2 tablespoons of oil for 1 minute. After the drying time is up, transfer the noodles to a large platter and sprinkle on the chopped scallions.

Cut the duck, with the bones, into bite-sized pieces. Each person should be served a bowl of noodles, a few pieces of duck, some vegetables from the platter, and a sprinkling of *nước chấm*.

NOTE

Instead of rice noodles, this dish can be served with French bread or Puffed Sweet or Glutinous Rice Balls (page 204). Achiote seeds are available in Oriental and Latin American groceries.

Duck with Sugar Cane

Vịt tiềm miá

8 servings

½ cup shelled peanuts, red skin removed
½ cup chestnuts, either fresh or dried
½ cup gingko nuts, canned or fresh
½ cup dried lotus seeds
8 dried Chinese mushrooms
½ cup red dates (jujubes)
1 duck (about 5 pounds)
Salt
1 tablespoon finely chopped fresh gingerroot

3 shallots, chopped fine
2 eighteen-inch pieces of sugar cane (if unavailable, omit)
Clear water from 1 coconut
1 teaspoon rock sugar
1 tablespoon fish sauce
3 scallions, both green part and white, cut into 4 pieces crosswise
Sprinkling of freshly ground black pepper
Sprig fresh coriander (Chinese parsley), chopped

Prepare the various nuts, the lotus seeds, dried mushrooms, and red dates as follows:

Soak the peanuts in hot water for 30 minutes; drain and set aside. If using dried chestnuts, boil for 20 minutes, drain, and set aside. If using fresh gingko nuts, remove the shell and blanch to remove the thin inner skin; set aside. Soak the Chinese mushrooms in hot water for 20 minutes, then drain, remove the stems and cut into quarters; set aside. Boil the dried lotus seeds for 20 minutes; drain and set aside. Soak the red dates in hot water for 30 minutes. (If they are very dry, boil for 10 minutes.) Drain and set aside.

Rinse and clean the duck. Rub salt over the duck and rinse off; let dry for 10 minutes.

Combine the ginger, shallots, and 1 teaspoon salt. Rub the inside of the duck with the mixture. Combine the peanuts, chestnuts, gingko nuts, lotus seeds, and 1 teaspoon salt and stuff the duck. Sew the duck closed with heavy white thread, or else use skewers.

Peel the sugar cane and cut into thin lengthwise strips, the same length as the duck. Place 3 pieces of white kitchen string on a flat surface, long enough to tie the slices of sugar cane around the duck, covering the entire surface. Bring the string around and tie as you would a roast. Turn the duck over and slide the remaining strips under the string, covering the entire duck with the sugar cane.

Pour the coconut water into a large pot. Put the duck into the pot and add enough water to completely cover. Add the rock sugar and 1 teaspoon of salt. Bring to a boil and remove the scum continuously for 15 minutes, then turn the heat down, cover, and keep at a lively bubble for 2 hours. Turn the duck every 30 minutes.

After 2 hours, remove the duck from the pot; untie and discard the sugar cane. To the liquid remaining in the pot add the mushrooms, red dates, 1 teaspoon salt, and the fish sauce. Boil, covered, for 15 minutes, then remove the duck to the broth, cover, and simmer for an additional 15 minutes. Remove the duck and add the scallion pieces to the broth.

To serve, break the duck, with the bones, into 8 pieces. Put the pieces in individual bowls and add broth, some of the various nuts that were stuffed into the duck, red dates, and mushrooms. Sprinkle with black pepper and chopped fresh coriander.

Duck Rice Soup
Cháo Vịt

After preparing this recipe, you have a complete dinner, with main course, soup, and fresh vegetable, and a delicious variation of our most frequently used *nước chấm* sauce—*nước chấm gừng*—to point up the flavors.

8 servings

1 duckling (4 to 4½ pounds),
  giblets and liver included
2½ quarts cold water
1 cup raw rice
1 teaspoon vegetable oil
2 tablespoons plus 1 teaspoon fish
  sauce (*nước mắm*)
Sprinkling of freshly ground
  black pepper

½ teaspoon salt
2 tablespoons shredded fresh
  gingerroot
2 tablespoons mixed chopped
  fresh coriander (Chinese
  parsley) and scallion green
Basic Vegetable Platter (pages
  37–38)
Ginger Fish Sauce (page 36)
  (*nước chấm gừng*)

Put the duck into a pot containing 2½ quarts of cold water, together with the giblets and liver. Bring to a boil, uncovered. Skim often, until all the scum is removed, and cook, uncovered, for 30 to 40 minutes over medium heat, bubbling gently, until the meat is tender. Remove the duck, liver, and giblets from the broth and set aside; measure 2 quarts of broth and pour into a pot.

Fry the rice in the oil over medium heat, stirring until the rice becomes transparent; this takes about 3 minutes. Add it to the soup, cover, and boil gently for 20 minutes. Then add the fish sauce, black pepper, and salt.

While the soup and rice are cooking, cut the duck in half lengthwise, then into thin crosswise slices, through the bones. Arrange on a platter. Cut the giblets and liver into thin slices and set aside.

To serve, pour the soup into individual bowls. Sprinkle into each bowl some of the giblet and liver, a few strips of ginger, and some of the coriander and scallions.

Each diner should be given an individual sauce dish containing ginger fish sauce, for dipping the duck and flavoring the soup if not sufficiently salty. The duck, after it is coated with sauce, is eaten with some of the lettuce, cucumber, coriander, and mint from the vegetable platter.

Fried Eggs with Pork and Onion
Chả Trứng Đúc Thịt

Another of Bạch's "lazy" dishes — quick and easy and tasty. Serve as part of a family dinner. It is best prepared in a nonstick pan.

4 servings

1 small onion
Freshly ground black pepper
2 teaspoons fish sauce (*nước mắm*)
2 tablespoons ground pork

2 teaspoons vegetable oil
1 clove garlic, chopped
2 eggs
1 tablespoon water

Cut the onion in half lengthwise, then into thin lengthwise strips.

Sprinkle some black pepper and 1 teaspoon of the fish sauce over the pork.

Heat the oil in a 7- or 8-inch frying pan. Add the garlic and stir, then add onion; fry briefly and add the meat. Stir continuously, breaking the meat into small pieces, until all traces of redness are gone.

Beat the eggs, then add 1 tablespoon water, remaining teaspoon of fish sauce, and a sprinkling of black pepper. Pour the eggs over the meat-onion mixture and cover. Turn the heat to low and check after about 3 minutes. When the eggs are cooked, the entire surface should look "set"; the pancake is turned over.

Serve with rice.

NOTE

This dish can be cooked using any amount of eggs you desire. You do not use a larger pan, you simply make a thicker pancake.

Fried Cabbage with Egg

Bắp Cải Xào Trứng

4 servings

1 egg
1 teaspoon fish sauce (*nước mắm*)
1 small cabbage (about 1 pound)
1 tablespoon vegetable oil
1 clove garlic, chopped

2 teaspoons water
Sprinkling of freshly ground black
  pepper
Dash of salt

Beat the egg and add the fish sauce. Shred the cabbage into thin strips 2 inches long.

Put the oil in a frying pan and heat over a high flame. Add garlic. Add the shredded cabbage; stir to coat with oil. Add the water, cover, and turn the heat down to medium. Uncover after 3 minutes and sprinkle with black pepper.

Make a well in the center of the cabbage. Pour in the beaten egg and stir, gradually combining the cabbage and egg. Sprinkle a little salt over all the ingredients and stir.

Serve with rice.

Steamed Egg and Mushrooms
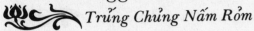 *Trứng Chửng Nấm Rơm*

4 servings

1 tablespoon vegetable oil
1 medium onion, sliced
5 straw mushrooms, sliced
2 tablespoons ground pork
4 eggs, beaten

2 teaspoons water
Sprinkling of freshly ground black
 pepper
2 teaspoons fish sauce (*nước mắm*)

Heat the oil in a frying pan. Add the onion and mushrooms and stir for about 2 minutes, then add the ground pork. Stir-fry until the pork loses its color.

Combine the beaten eggs with the water, freshly ground black pepper, and fish sauce; add the contents of the frying pan to the bowl of eggs. Transfer to a round Pyrex-type baking dish and steam over hot water for 5 minutes (see page 30).

NOTE

This recipe can also be fried. After frying the pork, add the egg mixture and cover for about 5 minutes, or until firm. Serve with rice.

Bamboo Shoot Omelet

Măng Làm Chả

The crisp bamboo shoots offer an interesting contrast in texture in this flavorsome dish.

4 servings

2 to 3 bamboo shoots
2 ounces ground pork
Sprinkling of freshly ground
   pepper
1 clove garlic, minced

Dash of granulated sugar
2 teaspoons fish sauce (*nước mắm*)
3 eggs
3 tablespoons vegetable oil

Cut the bamboo shoots into small shreds, 1 inch in length. Combine with the pork, black pepper, garlic, sugar, and ½ teaspoon of the fish sauce.

Beat the eggs and add the remaining 1½ teaspoons fish sauce. Then add the meat-bamboo shoot mixture to the eggs and mix well.

Heat the oil in a wok or deep 6-inch frying pan over a high flame. Measure ¼ cup of the egg mixture into a ladle and pour into the hot oil. Turn the heat down to medium. Keep the pancake thin and brown well, making sure the pork is well cooked. Before turning the pancake over, make certain that a brown crust is visible at the edge. (This amount of batter makes 4 pancakes.)

Serve with rice and Nước Chấm (page 34).

Fish and Seafood

Vietnam, with its fourteen hundred miles of shoreline, is a veritable mecca for seafood lovers. The rivers, too, teem with trout and carp — indeed, with fish of all varieties — and are an excellent source of freshwater fish for the Vietnamese kitchen.

Fish and shellfish of all kinds are relatively cheap, and appear on more Vietnamese tables than any of the meats. Sold directly as they are caught, the methods of preparation abound in inventiveness and ingenuity; the emphasis always on preserving the glorious fresh flavor and firm, resilient texture. Fish is eaten daily at lunch and dinner, and a meal will almost always include a fish dish.

Steamed Fish
Cà Hấp

The happy combination of condiments give this dish a seductively appealing flavor and fragrance. Steam this elegant-looking party dish in the dish on which it will be served, to keep it piping hot.

6 servings

1 whole mullet, sea bass, or blackfish (about 2 pounds), head and tail left on
¼ teaspoon salt
1 teaspoon granulated sugar
Sprinkling of freshly ground pepper
4 teaspoons fish sauce (*nước mắm*)
10 lily buds
3 Chinese mushrooms
½ ounce cellophane noodles, approximately
2 ounces fat pork shoulder

2 scallions, white part only, crushed and chopped
2 cloves garlic, chopped
1 teaspoon preserved vegetable (optional)
2 teaspoons shredded fresh gingerroot
1 celery stalk with leaves, cut horizontally into thin slices
1 onion, sliced
¼ cup sliced bamboo shoots
1 tomato, cut into 8 wedges

Wash and clean the fish well; dry with paper towels. Make 3 or 4 crosswise slashes on each side of the fish; then put into a dish with shallow sides, so that when it is steamed the liquid that accumulates will not be lost. Sprinkle over the fish the salt, sugar, black pepper, and fish sauce. Marinate for at least 30 minutes.

Meanwhile, in separate bowls, soak the lily buds, mushrooms, and cellophane noodles in warm water; the lily buds and cellophane noodles for 20 minutes and the mushrooms for 30 minutes.

Cut the pork into thin slices and then into narrow strips. Drop the pork shreds into the fish marinade and saturate with the liquid. Transfer the pork to the top of the fish.

Remove the lily buds from the water; remove the hard tip and tear each bud into 3 lengthwise strips with your fingers. Remove the stems from the soaked mushrooms and cut each one into 4 parts.

Arrange all the vegetables over the fish as attractively as possible with part of the tomato on top and the remainder around the fish. Drain the cellophane noodles and place on top of the vegetables.

Bring water to a boil in a steamer (see page 30) or a large roasting pan. (If you are using a roasting pan, put a high rack into the pot and place the fish platter onto the rack.) Turn the heat down to medium and cover; cook for 30 minutes. Keep covered until ready to serve.

Boneless Stuffed Whole Fish
Cá Rút Xửởng Đút Lò

This magnificent centerpiece will grace a most elaborate table.

6 servings

FISH

1 whole bluefish or sea bass (1½ pounds), head and tail left on
¼ teaspoon salt

Sprinkling of freshly ground black pepper
2 teaspoons vegetable oil

STUFFING

4 ounces ground pork
3 shallots or white part of 3 scallions, chopped
3 cloves garlic, chopped
1 small onion, chopped
1 tablespoon tree ears, soaked in warm water for 30 minutes, then rinsed, drained, and chopped fine

1 ounce cellophane noodles, soaked for 20 minutes in warm water, then drained and cut into 1-inch crosswise sections
1 egg yolk
¼ teaspoon salt

GARNISHES

2 hard-boiled eggs
2 lemons or limes
1 carrot, peeled and cut into strips

Sprigs of fresh coriander (Chinese parsley)

To bone the fish, open only the stomach side and detach the bone from the tail to the head, leaving head and tail attached. If you do not wish to bone the fish yourself, ask your fish dealer to do it. Sprinkle the salt and black pepper inside the fish, then combine all of the stuffing ingredients and fill the cavity of the fish with the mixture.

Preheat the oven to 350 degrees.

Line a baking pan with aluminum foil and place the fish on it. Sprinkle the oil over the fish and bake in the oven for 30 minutes.

To prepare the garnishes, cut the eggs and limes or lemons in half crosswise. Using the carrot strips, make handles and insert them to make baskets. Add some coriander leaves to the baskets.

Remove from the oven, decorate with the garnishes, and serve.

Fried Fish with Fresh Tomato Sauce

Cá Chiên Sốt Cà

When time runs short, here is a quick and savory treat.

4 servings

1 clove garlic
1 scallion, white part only
1 medium ripe tomato
¼ cup vegetable oil
1 slice bluefish or king mackerel
   (about ½ pound and ½ inch
   thick)

2 tablespoons fish sauce (*nước mắm*)
1 tablespoon granulated sugar
Sprinkling of freshly ground
   black pepper

Slice the garlic and scallion paper thin; combine and set aside. Cut the tomato into small dice and set aside.

In a small frying pan, just large enough to accommodate the fish slice, heat the oil over a high flame and add the fish. Turn the heat down to medium and fry the fish on either side until well browned. Remove to a warm platter.

Remove all the oil from the pan except for 2 teaspoons. Add the garlic and scallion and stir until brown. Add the diced tomato and stir; then add the fish sauce, sugar, and black pepper. Boil for 1 minute, stirring constantly, then pour over the fish and serve with rice.

Fried Fish Fillets with Sweet and Sour Sauce
Cá Lăn Bột Chiên Sốt Chua Ngọt

6 servings

1 clove garlic, chopped
½ onion, cut into thin lengthwise strips
1 entire scallion, cut into 2-inch lengths
1 carrot, peeled and sliced lengthwise with a carrot peeler
⅓ cup white radish, sliced lengthwise with a carrot peeler
1 small tomato, cut into 8 wedges
1 tablespoon thin soy sauce
2 teaspoons fish sauce (*nước mắm*)
½ teaspoon salt
2 tablespoons granulated sugar
1 tablespoon white vinegar
¼ cup plus 1 tablespoon cornstarch
Sprinkling of freshly ground black pepper
¾ cup water
¾ cup vegetable oil
1 pound fish fillets (bluefish, sole, or other)

Put all the vegetables in separate piles on a platter. Combine the soy sauce, fish sauce, salt, sugar, vinegar, 1 tablespoon cornstarch, black pepper, and water in a bowl.

Heat the oil in a 10-inch frying pan. Dip the fish fillets into the ¼ cup cornstarch and coat completely. Place in the hot oil and fry until brown on both sides; this should take about 5 to 8 minutes. Remove from the pan and set aside on a warm platter.

Remove all but 2 teaspoons of the oil from the pan. Turn the heat to high and add the chopped garlic, then stir for a few seconds and add the onion. Stir again and add the remaining vegetables. After they have cooked for an additional minute, restir the sauce mixture and pour it into the pan. Cook and stir for about 3 more minutes and pour over the fish.

Serve with rice.

Fried Fish

Cá Chiên

Quick cooking preserves the delicate freshness of these fish, and the *nước chấm* enhances the clear flavor.

4 servings

2 small, whole porgies or perch,
  heads and tails left on, or 2
  slices king mackerel or bluefish

½ cup vegetable oil
Nước Chấm (page 34)

If you are using the whole fish, cut Xs on either side of each, through the skin. Heat the oil and fry the fish on both sides until brown. Remove to a platter and pour the *nước chấm* over the fish before serving.

NOTE

It is not necessary to add any salt or other seasonings since the nước chấm *gives it sufficient flavor.*

Simmered Fish
Cá Kho Tộ

Deservedly famous throughout Vietnam, this savory delight from the South will win ecstatic comments. If catfish (pure white, firm meat) is not available, blackfish or halibut are fine. This is frequently served along with Sour Fish Head Soup (page 183).

4 servings

Sprinkling of freshly ground pepper
2 slices catfish, blackfish or halibut (about ½ pound)
3 tablespoons fish sauce (nước mắm)
2 tablespoons plus 1 teaspoon granulated sugar
1½ tablespoons vegetable oil

3 cloves garlic, chopped
5 shallots or white part of 5 scallions, sliced
2 ounces pork fat, sliced ½ inch thick and then into 2 × 1-inch pieces
2 tablespoons Caramelized Sugar (page 47; see note below)

Sprinkle black pepper over the fish slices, then add the fish sauce and sugar.

Heat 1 tablespoon of the oil in a small saucepan. Fry the garlic for a few seconds, then add about two-thirds of the shallots; stir and add the pork. Stir briefly and add the fish slices. Rotate the fish in the oil, back and forth and from one side to the other, to coat with oil and to sear; do this for about 3 minutes. Add the remaining sauce from the plate that contained the fish and fish sauce, then add the caramelized sugar. Turn the heat down to low and simmer, covered, for 10 minutes.

While the fish is simmering, heat the remaining oil (1½ teaspoons) in a small saucepan and brown the remaining shallots; after the fish has cooked for 10 minutes, add shallots to the simmering fish and cook for another 10 minutes, or until half the liquid has evaporated.

NOTE

Almost all simmered dishes, where fish sauce is used, contain caramelized sugar to enhance the appearance of the food.

Shrimp Pâté

Chả Tôm

Shrimp pâté is frequently served with Banana Leaf Cake (pages 212–13) and Nước Chấm (page 34). For a simpler alternative, serve with a bowl of rice, a Basic Vegetable Platter (pages 37–38), and *nước chấm*. It may also be served alone, as an appetizer, with drinks.

Although the original recipe calls for the use of a mortar and pestle, a food processor does an excellent job.

6 servings

1 pound raw shrimp, peeled and
    deveined
Salt
2 shallots
1 clove garlic
½ teaspoon granulated sugar
Dash of freshly ground black
    pepper

2 tablespoons pork fat, in a very
    small dice (about the size of
    peppercorns)
2 egg whites
1 egg yolk, slightly beaten

Peel and devein shrimp. Add ½ teaspoon salt to the cleaned shrimp. Mix well with your hands, then rinse the shrimp under cold running water. Dry well with paper towels.

Crush the shallots and garlic clove in a mortar. Add the shrimp and continue pounding until all the shrimp is reduced to a paste. (You may have to do this a little at a time if you do not own a large enough mortar and pestle; or reduce to a paste in a food processor then transfer to a bowl.) Add the sugar, black pepper, pork fat, egg whites, and salt to taste. Mix very well.

Oil a piece of aluminum foil about 6 inches square. Transfer the paste to the foil and pat it into a 5-inch square. Place it, in the foil, on a steamer rack above boiling water and cook, covered, for 15 minutes (see page 30). Uncover and paint the entire surface of the shrimp with slightly beaten egg yolk, then cook uncovered, for an additional 7 minutes. Remove and cut into 1-inch squares.

Serve as described above.

NOTE

This can be served at room temperature.

Shrimp Cakes
Bánh Tôm

6 servings

1 pound raw shrimp, shelled and
deveined
1½ cups all-purpose flour
1½ cups water
1¼ teaspoons salt
⅛ teaspoon freshly ground black
pepper

1 medium potato, peeled and cut
paper thin, then into very thin
shoestring slices
1½ cups vegetable oil

Wash the shrimp and dry well. Mash half of the shrimp to a paste using a mortar and pestle, a blender, or a food processor. Cut the remaining shrimp in half, lengthwise, and set aside.

Put the flour in a bowl and add the water gradually, stirring until smooth; the batter should have the consistency of thick cream. Add salt and pepper. Transfer the shrimp paste to the batter. Stir well to combine, then add the potato.

In a wok or deep saucepan, heat the oil to 375 degrees. With a round, shallow ladle, scoop up about 2 tablespoons of the batter. Place a whole shrimp in the batter in the ladle. Drop into the hot oil and fry for about 1 minute, then turn over. Fry until the batter is a light golden brown and the shrimp is pink, about 3 minutes in all. Serve hot or cold, with soft lettuce and Nước Chấm (page 34).

NOTE

In Vietnam, where the seafood is very fresh, the whole shrimp that is placed in the batter spoon is left unshelled.

Shrimp Toast

Bánh Mì Chiên Tôm

This is always served at a buffet. For shrimp toast lovers, the enhanced shrimp flavor and the crispness of the French bread combine with the *nước chấm* for a special treat.

6 servings

½ pound raw shrimp, in shell
1 egg white
2 tablespoons all-purpose flour
1½ teaspoons salt
½ teaspoon granulated sugar
⅛ teaspoon freshly ground black
  pepper

2 cloves garlic, chopped
2 scallions, both green and white
  parts, chopped
1 narrow loaf of French bread
1 cup vegetable oil

Peel and devein shrimp. Pulverize the shrimp to a paste with a mortar and pestle, a blender, or a food processor. Add the egg white, flour, salt, sugar, pepper, garlic, and scallions and stir well to combine.

Cut the French bread into slices ½ inch thick. Spread shrimp paste over one side of each slice.

Heat the oil in a frying pan to about 375 degrees. Drop in the bread slices, shrimp side down. Fry until the underside is brown, then turn over and brown the other side. Remove from the pan with a slotted spoon and drain on paper towels to remove excess fat.

Serve with lettuce leaves and Nước Chấm (page 34) as part of a party dinner or alone as an hors d'oeuvre.

Shrimp on Crab Legs

Càng Cua Bọc Tôm

Here we have a party dish that will bring out "oohs" and "ahs" from your guests on sight — and a repeat performance on taste.

Crab claws, alone, are sometimes available in fish stores. If they aren't, boil several hardshell crabs and use the claws; you can use the bodies in many other dishes.

The crab claws in fish stores are already partially peeled and serve not only as a handle but are edible as well. If you prepare your own claws, peel the upper section around which you mold the shrimp paste.

10 servings

10 crab legs or several hardshell   ¼ cup vegetable oil
  crabs
Shrimp paste, prepared as for
  Shrimp on Sugar Cane (pages
    67–68)

Boil the crab legs or crabs for about 10 minutes, then drain and cool; remove the claws from the crabs, if using, and reserve the bodies for another purpose.

Have the shrimp paste ready; preheat the oven to 350 degrees.

Pour the oil into a bowl. Dip your fingers into the oil and pick up 2 tablespoons of the shrimp paste. Mold it into an oval around and halfway down the crab claw, covering the part of the claw where it was attached to the body; this will leave a claw tip extended to serve as a handle. Place the claws on a baking sheet and bake in the preheated oven for 30 minutes.

Serve with Nước Chấm (page 34) and watercress.

NOTE

In Vietnam, this dish is always barbecued over charcoal. If you wish to prepare it this way, cook for 10 minutes on each side.

Shrimp Simmered in Fish Sauce

Tôm Rim

Shrimp enthusiasts — and there are very few people who aren't — will marvel at the rich flavor the fish sauce imparts to this dish.

4 servings

1 tablespoon vegetable oil
1 clove garlic, chopped
½ pound raw shrimp, shelled and deveined, tail section of shell left attached
3 tablespoons fish sauce (*nước mắm*)

1 tablespoon plus 1 teaspoon granulated sugar
2 teaspoons Caramelized Sugar (page 47)
Sprinkling of freshly ground black pepper

Heat the oil in a small saucepan over a high flame. Add the garlic and stir briefly, then add the shrimp. Turn the heat down to medium and continue to stir as you add the remaining ingredients — fish sauce, sugar, caramelized sugar, and pepper. After you have added these ingredients, cover the saucepan and continue to cook for 3 minutes. Uncover; half the liquid should have evaporated.

Serve with rice.

Crabs Farci

 *Cua farci*

6 servings

6 hard-shelled crabs
¼ pound ground pork
2 tablespoons tree ears, soaked
    for 20 minutes, then drained
    and chopped
1 small onion, chopped
1 ounce cellophane noodles,
    soaked 20 minutes, then
    drained and chopped

Sprinkling of freshly ground
    black pepper
1 egg, beaten
2 shallots, chopped
2 cloves garlic, chopped
2 teaspoons fish sauce (*nước mắm*)
¼ cup vegetable oil
1 bunch watercress

Break off the large claws from the crabs. Turn the crabs over and remove the roe, if the crab is female, and set aside.

Twist the skirt attached to the underside of each body. Break it off and discard. Also remove and discard the spongy parts attached to the crab. Rinse under cold running water. Remove the top shell from each; wash, dry well, and reserve for stuffing.

Cook the crab bodies for 5 minutes in boiling water. Drain and pick out the crabmeat, then combine with the reserved roe (if any), and the pork, tree ears, onion, cellophane noodles, pepper, egg, shallots, garlic, and fish sauce. Stuff the reserved crab shells with this mixture.

In a frying pan, heat the oil over a high flame. Place the crab shells in the oil, filling side down. Turn the heat to medium and cook until browned, then turn over and cook for 7 more minutes; the shells will turn bright orange.

To serve, arrange a bed of watercress on a platter and place crabs on it.

NOTE

Nước Chấm (page 34) can be served with this dish, but it is not a must. This is usually served as part of a party meal.

Stir-Fried Crabmeat with Cellophane Noodles
Cua Xaò Bún Taù

This combination of textures and flavor is irresistible — and very easy to prepare.

6 servings

1 package (3½ ounces) of cellophane noodles
2 tablespoons vegetable oil
1 clove garlic, chopped
2 shallots or white part of 2 scallions, chopped

6 ounces crabmeat, fresh or frozen
2 teaspoons fish sauce (*nuớc mắm*)
½ teaspoon freshly ground black pepper

Soak the cellophane noodles in warm water for 20 minutes. Remove from the water at least 30 minutes before cooking to allow them to dry, then cut into 4 crosswise sections.

Heat the oil in a frying pan over a high flame. Drop in the garlic and shallots and fry until golden brown, stirring constantly. Add the crabmeat and continue to fry and stir, still using high heat in order to remove moisture and dry the crabmeat. When the crabmeat is brown, add the noodles and stir a minute to combine. Add the fish sauce, stir, and serve immediately, with rice.

Vegetarian and Vegetable Dishes

The outdoor markets in Vietnam are notable for their enormous variety and abundance. The great heaps of vegetables, the brilliant color contrasts, and the exotic fragrances make a visit to these markets a memorable experience. Along with semitropical and tropical vegetables, many others associated primarily with the West's temperate climate, such as white potatoes and cauliflower, can be found. These vegetables, introduced by the French over the past hundred years, have been absorbed into Vietnamese cookery. They are grown around Dalat, a popular summer resort in the cool highlands of the mountainous Center.

At least two-thirds of the people of Vietnam are devout Buddhists, and their religion requires that on four days out of each month they eat only vegetables — no meat or seafood, not even fish sauce. Out of this rule, a rich and varied cuisine has developed, frequently simulating meat recipes with remarkable faithfulness.

Bean Curd

Đậu Khuông

Bean curd is so healthful and such a versatile ingredient, it is decidedly worthwhile making your own if it is not available. Unfortunately, most recipes don't work. (One could almost suspect the bean curd factory owners of seeing to it that it is a well-kept secret!) Bạch's recipe does work, and when the final product appears, you will have a warm sense of accomplishment.

When you make your own bean curd, plan in advance at least overnight or a similar period of time because you must make something called "sour water" before you can proceed with the final step.

SOUR WATER

6 ounces dried soybeans   ¼ cup white vinegar
1 quart water

Soak the dried soybeans in water to cover for at least 3 hours or as long as overnight. After they have soaked, drain off the water and rinse the beans. As you rinse, rub the beans between your hands; some of the husks will come off. Cover with water, drain and rinse and rub a few times, and most of the husk will separate from the beans. Some will remain attached (which should be of no concern). Drain one last time, discarding the water.

The soaked beans and 1 quart of water will now have to be combined in a blender. It will be necessary to do this in sections, as the blender does not have the capacity to accomplish this at one time. After all the beans and water, in equal parts each time, have been blended to a pulp (this is known as "soybean milk"), strain in a cheesecloth bag, again in sections, as follows:

Pour the bean milk into the bag and squeeze into a bowl, until all the liquid has been forced through the cheesecloth and only the pulp remains in the bag; discard the contents of the bag. Repeat this procedure until all the bean milk has been strained.

Transfer the liquid to a large pot over high heat. When the milk is just beginning to boil, add the vinegar and remove at once; it is not necessary to stir. Put the milk into a bowl and allow it to stand overnight, unrefrigerated and uncovered.

To continue the next day with the preparation of the bean curd, follow the initial instructions for the soaking, blending, and straining of the soybean milk, except that you should now use the following amounts:

1¼ pounds dried soybeans   4 quarts water

 Pour this larger amount of soybean milk into a very large pot, about 6 quarts in size, because it tends to boil over if the pot is not large enough. Turn the heat to high and stir gently for about 2 seconds to prevent the milk from boiling over. Allow the milk to come to a full boil, and when some bubbles appear and the liquid is just starting to boil, add all the sour water at once *without stirring*. Turn off the heat. When you add this water, the liquid will become very clear and a milky white mixture will float to the top; this is the bean curd.

Line a large colander with cheesecloth. Remove the skin or bean curd with a large spoon and place this in the cheesecloth-lined colander. Fold the cheesecloth over the bean curd into a square. The size does not matter; you will have a square of bean curd. Leave the wrapped bean curd in the colander; some of the liquid must be extracted.

Place a weight, such as a cutting board, a little larger in size than the bean curd square, on the bean curd. Press down hard with the weight until the water is drained; this will take a few minutes. Leaving the weight on top of the bean curd, allow it to cool for at least 20 minutes. (If the bean curd has not cooled sufficiently, it will break when removed from the colander.) After the bean curd cools, remove the cheesecloth package from the colander. Open it and cut the bean curd into the desired size.

Transfer to a bowl of cold water and refrigerate. The bean curd may be used immediately or stored for several days.

Bean Sprouts

The sprouts of mung beans will be found in all Oriental kitchens. Although they are increasingly available in the West, occasionally fresh bean sprouts may be hard to find. They do come in cans, but we find these unacceptable. So, if you can't find fresh bean sprouts, grow your own. Bear in mind that when they are fully grown (in about 4 days) the bean sprouts should be white and plump — about 2 inches long and ⅛ inch in diameter. They can be stored in cold water in the refrigerator for several days.

Start with as many mung beans as you wish, but ¼ cup will yield a generous crop, and after your first try you can decide for yourself exactly how much you wish to grow in the future.

Soak the beans overnight or for about 8 hours in a bowl of lukewarm water — they will swell quite a bit overnight — then drain off the water. Line a 2- to 3-quart glass or plastic bowl with damp paper towels or cheesecloth. Spread the beans over the towels, clustering them together. (We find that if the beans are clustered together, they stay moist, a condition essential to growth. If separated, they dry too quickly.) Wet another paper towel or more cheesecloth and cover the beans with it; then follow this procedure daily for 4 days: remove the top towel about 3 times a day, rinse or sprinkle the beans with water, drain the excess, and keep covered. If you feel that you might forget to water, hang a little sign in your kitchen saying: "Water the bean sprouts!" At first, the beans will roll around when you drain the water, but after a day they will start sending out roots, which will become embedded in the paper. Keep the bowl in a dark, warm place — in a closet, under the kitchen sink, or any other similar area.

After 4 days, when the bean sprouts are fully grown, transfer them to a bowl and fill with cold water. As the green husks float to the top, skim and discard them. (Separating them from the sprouts is well worth the effort. A conscientious Oriental cook — who has a lot of time — will remove each root from each bean sprout; but we don't recommend that you attempt this; it's time consuming, and might discourage you from growing a very worthwhile crop that has a multitude of uses.)

Vegetable Spring Rolls

Chả Giò Chay

Vegetable spring rolls must be very tightly wrapped, as there is no meat or binder in the filling to hold them together.

40 spring rolls

1 ounce cellophane noodles, soaked in warm water for 20 minutes, then drained and chopped fine

2 squares bean curd, finely chopped

3 small potatoes, peeled and cut paper thin with a carrot peeler, then shredded

1 tablespoon tree ears, soaked in warm water for 20 minutes, then drained and chopped

1 cup bean sprouts

1 medium carrot, peeled and cut paper thin with a carrot peeler, then cut into 1-inch sections and shredded

1 white part of leek, chopped

Sprinkling of freshly ground black pepper

10 dried rice papers (*bánh tráng*)

2 cups peanut oil

Make a filling by combining all the ingredients except the rice papers and oil. Cut or break the rice papers into quarters. Using a pastry brush or your fingers, wet the surface of each piece with water, and in about 1 minute the paper will become flexible and ready to be filled and rolled.

Place about 1 tablespoon of filling on each paper, following the directions for rolling spring rolls on page 59.

Heat the oil in a large frying pan, at least 10 inches in diameter, over a high flame to about 350 degrees. Using chopsticks, place the spring rolls in the oil, flap side down. When all the rolls are in the pan, reduce the heat to medium. Cook for 20 minutes, 10 minutes on each side, until completely brown.

Serve with Buddhist Nước Lèo (page 36) or soy sauce.

Buddhist Monk's Soup

Canh Kiểm

Buddhist Monk's Soup is enormously popular. There can be no sense of deprivation because this dish, with its flavorful ingredients magnificently enhanced by the coconut milk, is a remarkably good source of high-quality protein, and it will stick to your ribs.

6 servings

1 quart water
1 pound pumpkin or butternut
squash, peeled and cut into
large chunks
1 sweet potato, peeled and cut
into chunks
½ cup raw peanuts, shelled and
red skin removed, soaked for
30 minutes then drained and
roughly chopped
⅓ cup dried mung beans, soaked
for 30 minutes and drained

3 tablespoons vegetable oil
1 square bean curd
1 quart coconut milk, fresh (see
page 48) or canned (see note
below)
½ ounce cellophane noodles,
soaked for 20 minutes, then
drained and cut into 1-inch
crosswise sections

Bring the water to a boil. Drop in the pumpkin or squash, sweet potato, peanuts, and mung beans. Cook over medium heat for 35 minutes.

While the soup is cooking, prepare the bean curd. Heat the oil in a small frying pan and fry the bean curd on both sides until light brown. Slice lengthwise into strips ¼ inch wide and reserve until needed.

After 35 minutes of cooking, check to make certain that the mung beans are soft. If they are, add the coconut milk. Add salt. Bring to a boil and drop in the cellophane noodles and fried bean curd. Serve with rice and Buddhist Nướć Lèo (see page 36).

NOTE

If using canned coconut milk, add enough water to the contents of a 12-oz. can to equal 1 quart of coconut milk. Raw peanuts, with outer shells and inner red skins already removed, can be purchased in Oriental groceries.

Bean Curd-Stuffed Tomato

 *Cà Chua Dồn Đậu Hủ*

4 servings

4 medium tomatoes
1 square bean curd, mashed to a
   paste
¼ cup straw mushrooms
2 tablespoons cellophane noodles,
   soaked in warm water for 20
   minutes, then drained and
   chopped finely

White part of ½ leek, chopped
Sprinkling of freshly ground
   black pepper
½ teaspoon salt
¼ teaspoon granulated sugar
2 tablespoons vegetable oil

Remove and discard the tops and pulp of the tomatoes. Combine the remaining ingredients, except for the oil, and stuff into tomatoes.

Heat the oil in a frying pan over a high flame. Put the tomatoes in the pan, stuffed side down, then turn the heat down to medium and cover. Fry until brown, about 3 minutes; turn over and fry for about 3 minutes more. Remove from heat.

Serve with either Buddhist Nước Lèo (page 36) or thin soy sauce.

Bean Curd Simmered with Vegetables and Coconut Milk

Đậu Hủ Kho Nước Dừa

6 servings

½ cup vegetable oil, approximately
1 pound bean curd (about 5
  squares), cut into 1-inch cubes
1 two-inch piece white part of
  leek, sliced thin
1 cup small cauliflower florets
20 string beans, strings removed
  and cut in half

1 cup coconut milk, fresh or
  canned
½ cup water
1 teaspoon salt
1 tablespoon black soy sauce
1 teaspoon granulated sugar

Put enough oil in a frying pan to reach a depth of ½ inch. Heat the oil over a high flame, then fry the bean curd cubes until browned on all sides. Remove the bean curd from pan and drain on paper towels.

Remove all but 2 teaspoons of the oil from the pan. Drop in the leek and stir until it is lightly browned, then add the cauliflower and string beans and fry until the vegetables are coated with oil. Return the fried bean curd to the pan, stir for a minute, and add the remaining ingredients. Stir, cover, and simmer for about 10 minutes, until the string beans and cauliflower are tender.

Serve with rice.

Cauliflower with Straw Mushrooms

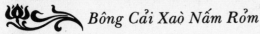 *Bông Cải Xaò Nấm Rởm*

4 servings

1 cup cauliflower florets
1 leek, white part only
1 tablespoon soy sauce
2 tablespoons water

¼ teaspoon granulated sugar
1 tablespoon vegetable oil
½ cup straw mushrooms

Cut the cauliflower florets into thin lengthwise slices; slice the leek horizontally into thin slices. Place in separate bowls.

Measure the soy sauce, 1 tablespoon water, and sugar into a bowl. Heat the oil in a frying pan over a high flame. Drop in leek and stir briefly, then add the cauliflower. Stir some more. Add remaining 1 tablespoon of the water and cover, then turn the heat down to medium and cook for 2 minutes. Uncover and add the straw mushrooms and sauce mixture. Cover and cook for 2 more minutes, then remove from the heat and serve with rice.

Cabbage Fried with Cellophane Noodles and Bean Curd

Bắp Su Xaò Bún Taù

4 to 6 servings

5 tablespoons vegetable oil
1 square bean curd
1 leek, white part only, chopped
1 cup string beans, halved
1 pound cabbage, sliced ¼ inch
  thick

2 ounces cellophane noodles,
  soaked in warm water for 20
  minutes, then drained and cut
  into 4 pieces
½ teaspoon salt
Sprinkling of freshly ground
  black pepper

Heat 3 tablespoons of the oil over a high flame. Fry the bean curd until lightly browned on both sides, then remove from the pan and cut lengthwise into slices ½ inch thick. Set aside.

Heat the remaining 2 tablespoons oil in another pan. Add the leek and fry for 1 minute, then add the string beans and cabbage; stir and cover. Reduce the heat to medium and cook for 5 minutes. Uncover and add the cellophane noodles, salt, and pepper. Stir well and cover for an additional 5 minutes. Uncover, add the bean curd, and stir for 1 minute more.

Serve with rice.

Puffed Eggplant

Cà Dê Phích Bột

6 servings

1 small eggplant (½ pound)
1½ cups all-purpose flour
2 eggs, slightly beaten
1 cup water

Dash of salt
Sprinkling of freshly ground
    pepper
¾ cup vegetable oil

Peel the eggplant and cut in half lengthwise, then into slices ¼ inch thick.

Make a batter by combining the flour and eggs. Gradually add the water, a little at a time. Mix well and add salt and pepper.

Heat the oil in a wok or frying pan over a high flame. When very hot, reduce the heat to medium (about 375 degrees; see note below). Dip the eggplant in the batter and drop, one piece at a time, into the hot oil; fry until light brown on both sides. Drain each piece as it comes out of the pan on paper toweling.

Serve with rice and Nước Chấm (page 34).

NOTE

It is important that the oil temperature be kept at about 375 degrees. If it gets too hot, the batter will cook too quickly and the eggplant will remain uncooked.

Soups and Fondues

The soups of Vietnam present an almost bewildering variety. They range from thin soups to hearty, thick ones, delicate in flavor and aroma to pungent, substantial dishes that are often a full meal in themselves (see the chapter on noodles and noodle soups, pages 217–28). They are generally served over rice and garnished on the side with coriander and wedges of lime. If additional salt is desired, a dash or so of fish sauce (*nước mắm*) will bring the desired level of saltiness to your taste.

All fondues are party dishes served on festive occasions. The cooking time is very short, and the diners do the actual cooking.

Soup with Cabbage Pork Rolls

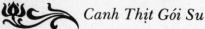 *Canh Thịt Gói Su*

A delight to the eye as well as the palate, the little packages of meat, wrapped in cabbage leaves and tied with dainty green scallion bows, will be an instant success. This is generally served as part of a family dinner.

6 servings

15 large outer leaves of cabbage
3 cups water or stock (see page 49)
10 scallions, green part only
½ pound ground pork
4 ounces ground beef
2 tablespoons plus 2 teaspoons
   fish sauce (*nước mắm*)
1 clove garlic, finely chopped

Freshly ground black pepper
1 shallot or white part of 1 scallion
½ teaspoon salt
Dash of MSG (optional)
2 tablespoons mixed chopped
   fresh coriander (Chinese
   parsley) and scallion green
6 cups cooked rice (see page 41)

Cut the cabbage leaves in half, removing the tough center seams. Bring the water to a boil and drop in the cabbage leaves. Remove from the boiling water after 3 minutes and set aside; drop the whole scallion greens into the boiling water and remove instantly. Setting the water aside for use later, cut the scallion greens in half lengthwise to make long, thin strings.

Combine the ground pork, ground beef, 2 teaspoons fish sauce, garlic, ⅛ teaspoon black pepper, and the shallots. Mix well with your hands.

Fill each cabbage leaf with 2 teaspoons of the meat mixture. Shape into a cylinder 2 inches across the wide part of the leaf. Fold the sides over to enclose the meat and roll as for spring rolls (see page 59). Tie a scallion string around the center of each cabbage roll.

Bring the reserved water to a boil. Add the 2 tablespoons fish sauce, salt, and MSG and drop the cabbage rolls into the boiling liquid. Boil gently, at medium heat, for 15 minutes, partially covered.

To serve, transfer the soup to a tureen and sprinkle on top the chopped coriander and scallion and some black pepper. Fill individual bowls two-thirds full of rice. Add soup until it comes up to the level of the rice; then place some cabbage rolls on top. The remaining soup and cabbage rolls can remain in the tureen for additional servings.

This soup can also be served without rice.

Stuffed Squash Soup

Canh Squash

There are many varieties of squash in Vietnam not available in the West. However, the butternut squash used in this recipe is an excellent substitute.

6 servings

STOCK

6 cups water
1 to 2 pounds beef or pork bones (see note below)
1 tablespoon fish sauce (*nước mắm*)

1 teaspoon salt
1 beef bouillon cube

STUFFED SQUASH

1 butternut squash (about 1½ pounds)
4 ounces ground pork
2 shallots, or white part of 2 scallions, chopped

1 clove garlic, chopped
Sprinkling of freshly ground black pepper
1 teaspoon fish sauce (*nước mắm*)

GARNISH

2 tablespoons mixed chopped fresh coriander (Chinese parsley) and scallion green

First start the stock. Bring the water to a boil. Add the bones and boil for 45 minutes. During this 45-minute period, make the following preparations:

Cut the squash in half horizontally, separating the neck from the lower bowl-shaped part. Remove the seeds from the bowl and peel the entire squash. Cut the neck part into quarters lengthwise, and then into slices ¼ inch thick. Dry the inside of the bowl with a paper towel.

Combine the pork with the shallots and garlic. Sprinkle on the black pepper and fish sauce, then fill the squash bowl with the meat mixture; make small meatballs if there is any meat remaining.

After the 45-minute cooking period is over, add to the stock the meat-filled squash bowl (meat side down) as well as the sliced squash and meat-

balls. Cook, covered, for 10 minutes, then turn the squash bowl meat side up and cook for another 15 minutes, covered. Uncover and add the fish sauce, salt, and bouillon cube.

Transfer to a soup tureen and sprinkle with the fresh coriander and scallion green. Serve with a bowl of Nước Chấm (page 34) which each diner can sprinkle over to taste.

NOTE

If no bones are available, substitute a 13-ounce can of beef broth and 2 soup cans of water in place of the 6 cups of water and bones.

Taro Soup with Ground Pork

Canh Khoai Môn Thịt Heo

Taro is a somewhat sticky, potatolike root vegetable. In Vietnam there are many varieties — purple, white, yellow, ranging in size from tiny to large, all with different flavors. Hawaiian *poi*, fabled in song and story, is made from taro. While we in the West do not have the many varieties to choose from, taro root is easily obtainable in Oriental or Latin American groceries. This recipe is a hearty example of how it is used.

6 servings

SOUP

6 ounces ground pork
2 scallions, white part only, chopped
⅛ teaspoon freshly ground black pepper

1 tablespoon plus 1 teaspoon fish sauce (*nước mắm*)
1 pound taro root
1 quart water
1 teaspoon salt

GARNISH

1 tablespoon chopped fresh coriander (Chinese parsley)

2 scallion greens, chopped

Combine the pork, scallions, pepper, and 1 teaspoon fish sauce and shape into 1-inch meatballs.

Peel the taro and slice ½ inch thick or, if you like, "slice" Vietnamese fashion, which is not really slicing, as follows: after peeling, using a rounded 1-inch measuring spoon, scoop out pieces. (This is similar to using a melon baller, except that the pieces are shallower in depth and wider over all.)

Bring the water to a boil. Drop in the meatballs and taro and cook at a boil for 15 minutes. After 15 minutes, test to make certain the taro is soft; if not, cook a few minutes more. When the taro is ready, add 1 tablespoon fish sauce and 1 teaspoon salt to the soup.

Sprinkle with the coriander and scallion greens and serve with rice.

Papaya Soup with Pork Hock

Canh Giò Heo Đu Đủ

Traditionally, papaya soup is an important part of the diet for women after childbirth. It is felt that they will have more milk to feed their babies and will regain their strength more rapidly. Bach, after each of her four children were born, had papaya soup every day for a month, as did her mother for each of her eleven children.

Incidentally, childbirth is not a prerequisite for the enjoyment of this richly satisfying soup.

4 servings

4 cups water plus 2 cups chicken
  stock
4 slices fresh pork hock, each 1
  inch thick
1 green papaya, cut into 1-inch
  cubes (or enough to make 2
  cups)

4 teaspoons fish sauce (*nước mắm*)
Salt to taste
Sprinkling of freshly ground
  black pepper
1 sprig fresh coriander (Chinese
  parsley), chopped
Chopped scallion green

Bring the 6 cups of liquid to boil in a 2-quart pot. Drop in the pork hock and cook for 15 minutes, removing the scum several times during the cooking period; this procedure will keep the stock clear. After 15 minutes of skimming and boiling, cover the pot, reduce the heat to medium, and cook for an additional hour, or until the pork hock becomes tender. At this point, the liquid should be reduced to approximately 4 cups.

Add the papaya and cook for an additional 15 minutes, then add the fish sauce and salt. Stir, remove from the heat, and transfer to a tureen. Sprinkle with black pepper, coriander, and chopped scallion green.

This soup should be served over rice or plain, as part of a family dinner.

Beef Soup with Pineapple and Tomato
Canh Cà Chua Thơm Thịt Bò

This unusual combination — for Western tastes — of fresh pineapple with tomato blends with the seasonings for a bright, mouth-filling flavor.

6 servings

6 ounces beef shoulder or round, in 1 chunk

Sprinkling of freshly ground black pepper

1 tablespoon fish sauce (*nước mắm*)

1-inch slice fresh pineapple

1 medium tomato

1 shallot or scallion, white part only

1 tablespoon vegetable oil

3 cups water

1 beef bouillon cube

½ teaspoon salt

2 tablespoons mixed chopped coriander (Chinese parsley) and scallion green

Slice the beef thin. Sprinkle with black pepper and 2 teaspoons of the fish sauce and marinate for 30 minutes.

Cut the pineapple slice into thin crosswise slices. Cut the tomato into 8 wedges. Slice the shallot thin. Arrange all the vegetables in separate mounds on a platter and set aside.

Heat the oil in a 2-quart saucepan. Add the sliced shallot, the pineapple, and tomato and fry for about 1 minute, stirring continuously. Add the meat and stir, and then, when the meat is half cooked, add the water and bring to a boil. Add the beef bouillon cube, salt, and remaining 1 teaspoon fish sauce.

Sprinkle the coriander and scallion green over the soup just before serving; serve with rice.

Beef Soup with Lemon Grass

 *Canh Thịt Bò Xáo Sả*

As a young girl, Bach learned this recipe from her mother. The aroma and flavor of the lemon grass give this soup its unique character.

6 servings

1 stalk fresh lemon grass or 1 tablespoon dried
Sprinkling of freshly ground black pepper
2 teaspoons fish sauce (*nước mắm*)
1 clove garlic, chopped
6 ounces fatty beef chuck, sliced paper thin
1 teaspoon vegetable oil

2 shallots or white part of 2 scallions, sliced
3 cups water
1½ beef bouillon cubes
1 teaspoon salt
1 tablespoon fresh coriander (Chinese parsley), chopped
2 scallions, green part only, chopped

If you are using fresh lemon grass, simply remove the outer leaves and upper two-thirds of the stalk, then chop. If you are using dried, it must be soaked for 2 hours, then drained and chopped fine.

Sprinkle the black pepper, 1 teaspoon of the fish sauce, and chopped garlic over the meat; mix well and allow the meat to absorb the flavors for a few minutes.

Heat the oil and fry the shallots over a high flame. Add the lemon grass and fry for about 1 minute, then add the meat. Cook until all traces of redness are gone. Add the water, bring to a boil, and add the beef bouillon cubes, remaining 1 teaspoon fish sauce, and salt.

Immediately before serving, bring the soup to a boil. Pour into bowls and sprinkle with the chopped coriander and scallion.

Beef Rice Soup
Cháo Thịt Bò

This is the final dish served at the Beef in Seven Dishes restaurants we mentioned in the recipe for Beef Fondue with Vinegar on pages 184–85.

6 servings

½ cup plus 1 tablespoon vegetable oil
½ cup raw rice
5½ cups water
6 ounces ground beef
7 teaspoons fish sauce (*nước mắm*)
Freshly ground black pepper
2 tablespoons chopped onion

½ ounce cellophane noodles
2 tablespoons Roasted Peanuts (page 46), chopped
1 tablespoon chopped fresh coriander (Chinese parsley)
1 tablespoon chopped scallion green

Heat the tablespoon oil, then add the rice and stir until the rice becomes transparent; add the water and bring to a boil. Continue to boil, half covered, until the rice is tender, about 15 minutes.

While the rice is boiling, combine the meat with 2 teaspoons of the fish sauce, a sprinkling of black pepper, and the chopped onion. Set aside.

Heat the ½ cup of oil to about 375 degrees in a small saucepan. With your hands, loosen the cellophane noodle strands and add to the heated oil. Fry until they puff up, which should take about 30 seconds. (The noodles should not brown in the oil; they just become a milky white color when they puff.) Remove from the oil with a slotted spoon and crumble the noodles into small pieces. Set aside.

When the rice has become tender, add the marinated ground beef in one lump, stirring briskly to separate into small pieces; continue to stir for 3 minutes. Add the remaining fish sauce, black pepper, and the noodles. Sprinkle with chopped peanuts, coriander, and scallion green before serving.

Chicken Soup with Lily Buds and Cellophane Noodles

Canh Kim Châm Bún Taù

Bạch calls this a "lazy" dish. It takes only a few minutes to prepare, and is usually served with rice as part of the family dinner.

6 servings

20 lily buds
1 ounce cellophane noodles
3¼ cups fresh chicken broth or 1 can (13¾ ounces) chicken broth plus 1½ cups cold water
1 chicken leg

1 tablespoon fish sauce (*nước mắm*)
Sprinkling of freshly ground black pepper
2 tablespoons mixed chopped fresh coriander (Chinese parsley) and scallion green

In separate bowls, soak the lily buds and cellophane noodles in warm water for about 20 minutes.

Place the chicken broth in a saucepan. Place the chicken leg in the cold broth and bring to a boil. Turn the heat down to medium, cover, and cook for 15 to 20 minutes, uncovering from time to time to remove scum from the surface of the soup.

Remove the chicken leg from the broth; take the meat from the bone and shred with your hands. Return the shredded chicken to the broth.

Remove the noodles from the water and cut into 3 crosswise sections. Remove the hard tip from each lily bud and tie a single knot in each (this enhances the appearance). Add the lily buds to the broth and stir, then add the noodles, fish sauce, and a sprinkling of black pepper. Bring to a boil and turn off immediately. Sprinkle with the chopped coriander and scallion just before serving.

Soup with Bok Choy and Cellophane Noodles
Canh Cải Bún Taù

When you are feeling lazy, you'll find this family dinner dish fast and easy to prepare. Serve with rice.

6 servings

1 ounce cellophane noodles
2 stalks *bok choy*
1 quart chicken stock, homemade
(see note below) or canned (1
thirteen-ounce can plus 2½
cups water)

2 tablespoons fish sauce (*nướ́c
mắ́m*)

Soak the cellophane noodles in warm water for 20 minutes. Cut the *bok choy* into 2-inch pieces.

Pour the broth into a saucepan and add the fish sauce.

Drain the cellophane noodles and cut the strands into 3 crosswise sections. Add, along with the *bok choy*, to the soup. Bring to a boil and serve immediately. If you wish to serve later, drop the *bok choy* and cellophane noodles into the soup and turn the heat off; when you are ready to serve, bring to a boil.

NOTE

If you are using homemade broth, add 1 teaspoon salt.

Creamed-Corn Chicken Soup

Bắp Hộp Nấu Gà

This recipe gives a traditional Western soup a delightful piquancy. Besides that, it is fast and easy and can be cooked ahead, refrigerated, and reheated.

6 to 8 servings

1½ cups chicken broth, fresh or
   canned
1 quart water
1 pound chicken legs with thighs
2 teaspoons salt
2 teaspoons fish sauce (*nửớc mắm*)
1 can (15 ounces) creamed corn

1 teaspoon vegetable oil
1 clove garlic, chopped
1 tablespoon white wine
1 egg
Sprinkling of freshly ground
   black pepper

Put the chicken broth and water in a kettle; add the chicken legs and thighs to cold liquid, then bring to a boil and cook over medium heat, covered, for 20 minutes. Turn off flame. Remove the chicken. Shred and add it to the broth with the salt, fish sauce, and creamed corn.

Heat the oil in a small pan. Add garlic and stir, then add the wine, stir a few seconds, and immediately add to broth. Return to a boil and break the egg into the soup; stir and remove from the heat. Sprinkle with black pepper and serve.

Shrimp Rice Soup

Cháo Tôm

6 to 8 servings

1 cup raw rice
½ pound raw shrimp, shelled and deveined
2 tablespoons plus 1 teaspoon fish sauce (*nước mắm*)
Sprinkling of freshly ground black pepper
3 shallots or white part of 3 scallions

1 tablespoon vegetable oil
1 clove garlic, chopped
2 quarts pork stock or water
¼ teaspoon salt
2 tablespoons chopped fresh coriander (Chinese parsley)
2 tablespoons chopped scallion green

Pound the rice in a mortar to break it, or put it in a blender for 8 seconds. Cut the shrimp in half lengthwise. Wash and dry the shrimp, then cut each half into 4 crosswise pieces. Sprinkle the 1 teaspoon fish sauce, pepper, and shallots over the shrimp and mix well.

Heat the oil in a large pot; add the garlic and let it brown, then add the shrimp; stir-fry for 3 minutes. Add the stock, cover, and bring to a boil. Add the rice to the stock and cook, partially covered, until soft — about 15 minutes. Add the 2 tablespoons fish sauce and salt and remove from the heat. Transfer to a tureen and sprinkle coriander, scallion, and black pepper over the soup before serving.

Asparagus Crab Soup

Súp Măng Tây Cua

The French introduced asparagus to the Vietnamese, who promptly incorporated this classic vegetable into their cuisine. The Vietnamese word for asparagus is "Western bamboo," due to its resemblance to bamboo shoots. Universally popular throughout Vietnam, this light, tasty dish will delight your family as well.

6 to 8 servings

2½ quarts water
2 pounds pork bones
2 teaspoons salt
1 tablespoon fish sauce (nước mắm)
1 teaspoon vegetable oil
1 clove garlic, chopped
2 shallots or white part of 2 scallions, chopped
½ pound crabmeat, fresh, frozen, or canned

¼ teaspoon freshly ground black pepper
2 teaspoons cornstarch dissolved in 2 tablespoons water
1 egg
1 can (15 ounces) white asparagus, undrained
¼ cup chopped fresh coriander (Chinese parsley)
¼ cup chopped scallion green

Bring water to a boil and put the pork bones in. Remove the scum, then cover and continue to boil the bones for 1 hour. Remove the bones from the stock and discard. Add the salt and the fish sauce to the stock.

Heat the oil and add the chopped garlic and shallots; add the crabmeat and fry for 5 minutes over high heat. Sprinkle with ⅛ teaspoon of black pepper, stirring constantly, then add the crabmeat mixture to the soup and bring to a boil. Add the cornstarch-and-water mixture and stir for a few minutes.

Break the egg open and drop it into the actively boiling soup while stirring. Cook, still stirring, for about 2 minutes, then drop in the asparagus, along with the liquid from the can and the rest of the black pepper. Continue to cook until the asparagus is heated through. Sprinkle the coriander and scallion green over the soup before serving.

Sour Fish Head Soup
Canh Chua Đầu Cá

An excellent way to get twice the pleasure out of your fish purchase. You can use either the fish head or the fish carcass if you wish. To the people of the South, this is as much their traditional dish as Southern Fried Chicken is to our southerners — and it will meet with instant praise.

4 servings

2 scallions, white part only, crushed with the side of a knife
Sprinkling of freshly ground black pepper
2 teaspoons salt
2 tablespoons plus 4 teaspoons fish sauce (*nước mắm*)
1 large fish head or fish carcass, split down the center

1 quart water
½ cup canned sliced sour bamboo
¼ fresh pineapple, cut in a lengthwise section and sliced
Dash of MSG (optional)
2 tablespoons mixed chopped fresh coriander (Chinese parsley) and scallion green

Sprinkle the scallions, black pepper, 1 teaspoon salt, and 4 teaspoons fish sauce over the fish head. Allow to stand for 10 to 15 minutes.

Bring 1 quart of water to a boil and drop in the sour bamboo and pineapple slices. Cook at a lively boil for 5 minutes. Drop the fish head into the actively boiling water and, keeping at a boil, add the 2 tablespoons fish sauce, remaining teaspoon salt, and a dash of MSG. Boil the fish head for a total of 10 minutes. Transfer to a soup tureen, sprinkle on the coriander and scallion green, and serve.

NOTE

If the fish head is dropped into water that is not boiling, it will fall apart.

Beef Fondue with Vinegar

Bò Nhúng Dấm

In Saigon, there are several restaurants specializing in Beef in Seven Dishes (*Bò Bảy Món*), and when one is planning to go to one of them, rather than mentioning the name of the restaurant, one simply says that one is "going to Beef in Seven Dishes."

The most famous of these restaurants, Ánh Hồng (named after the owner's favorite racehorse), is owned by a friend of Bach's and her husband's.

The first dish that is served in this meal is always this one, Beef Fondue with Vinegar and the last is always Beef Rice Soup (page 177).

6 servings

BEEF PLATTER

¾ pound beef fillet or other lean, tender beef, in 1 chunk
Freshly ground black pepper
1 tomato

1 tablespoon vegetable oil
1 onion
White vinegar

SAUCE

2 cloves garlic
2 tablespoons granulated sugar
1 fresh hot red chili pepper
1 can (2 ounces) flat anchovies, including oil

1 tablespoon fish sauce (*nước mắm*)
Juice of ½ lime
1 tablespoon water

FONDUE BROTH

1 tablespoon vegetable oil
1 clove garlic, chopped
1 teaspoon tomato paste

½ cup white vinegar
2 cups water
1 tablespoon granulated sugar

ACCOMPANIMENTS FOR SERVING

12 dried rice papers (*bánh tráng*)

Basic Vegetable Platter (pages 37–38)

Slice the beef paper thin and arrange in overlapping slices on a platter. Sprinkle liberally with black pepper. Slice the tomato thin and arrange over beef. Sprinkle oil over all.

Slice the onion in half lengthwise, then into thin crosswise slices. Cover with white vinegar in a bowl and marinate for 3 to 5 minutes. Drain and discard the vinegar and arrange the onion over the tomatoes and meat, separating into half rings. Set aside while you make the sauce.

In a mortar, pound 1 clove of the garlic, the sugar, and red chili pepper to a smooth paste. Add the anchovies and mash well. Add the fish sauce and lime juice, stirring constantly to a smooth paste. Add the water and mix well. Mince the remaining garlic clove and sprinkle over the sauce. Set aside.

To make the fondue broth, heat the oil in a saucepan. Add the garlic and tomato paste, then stir and add the vinegar, water, and sugar. Bring to boil and transfer to a fondue pot.

To serve, put the dried rice papers, cut into quarters, on a platter. Place a shallow soup bowl of water near each diner, then place the vegetable platter and meat platter on the table. Give each person a small dish of sauce; heat the fondue broth.

Each diner takes a rice paper and dips it briefly into the water bowl, which will soften it instantly and make it pliable. He then places some of the vegetables on the paper, after which he takes a few slices of meat, a slice of onion, and a slice of tomato, and drops them into the boiling fondue liquid for about a minute. He then transfers these to the rice paper and rolls it into a narrow cylinder shape. The "package" should then be dipped into the individual sauce bowl and eaten out of hand.

NOTE

The beef platter and sauce can be prepared up to a half day ahead. The beef should be covered with plastic wrap and be refrigerated.

Beef, Shrimp, and Fish Fondue with Coconut Water

Lâũ Thập Cẩm

This recipe wins on three counts: it is excellent for do-ahead cooking, the combination of seafood and meat cooked in coconut-water broth will bring you unstinted praise, and it is as beautiful to the eye as it is to the taste. A superb party dish.

6 servings

FOOD PLATTER

4 ounces beef fillet, sliced paper thin

4 ounces blackfish or any white-fleshed fish, sliced paper thin

5 large raw shrimp, peeled and deveined, then cut in half lengthwise

1 tomato, thinly sliced

1 onion, thinly sliced

Sprinkling of freshly ground black pepper

1 tablespoon sesame oil

SAUCE

Clear water from 1 coconut (see page 14)

2 tablespoons distilled white vinegar

2 teaspoons vegetable oil

2 shallots, chopped

2 cloves garlic, chopped

1 teaspoon tomato paste

1 teaspoon salt

2 teaspoons granulated sugar

½ cup water

ACCOMPANIMENTS FOR SERVING

Nước Chấm (page 34)

Dried rice papers (*bánh tráng*)

Basic Vegetable Platter (pages 37–38)

Arrange the meat, fish, and shrimp on a large platter in separate sections. Place the sliced tomato and onion over the meat and fish. Sprinkle the black pepper and sesame oil over all and set aside while you prepare the sauce.

Combine the coconut water with the vinegar and set aside.

Heat the vegetable oil over a high flame, then add the chopped shallots and garlic and brown lightly. Add the tomato paste and stir to combine well. Pour the coconut water mixture into the saucepan containing the shallots and garlic and add the salt, sugar, and water. Bring to a boil and transfer to a fondue pot with a heating unit and bring it to the table, along with the food platter.

To serve, give each person partaking of the food a flat plate and a small bowl of *nước chấm* for dipping. Each one of them takes a round sheet of dried rice paper, completely coating it with water with the fingers. While the softening effect of the water is taking place, each diner drops a piece of beef, shrimp, fish, onion, and tomato into the bubbling liquid very briefly, then removes the food and transfers it to the rice paper, placing on top of the assortment a little of each vegetable from the vegetable platter. Then each rice paper should be folded over, to enclose the sides, and rolled up (see the diagram for spring rolls on page 59). The package is then dipped into *nước chấm* and eaten, a process that is repeated after each bite.

Beef Fondue with Shrimp Sauce

Thịt Bò Bà Lai Chanh

This is a very popular dish from the famous Sinh Sinh Restaurant in Saigon. After having it there at least once a month, Bach was able to reproduce it at home, and it has become a family favorite. The combination of shrimp sauce and lemon grass is typical of the exciting combinations to be found in this exotic cuisine.

This can be a one-dish meal or served as part of a larger dinner. All preliminary preparation for this dish can be done up to six hours before serving.

6 servings

BEEF PLATTER

6 scallions
1 pound beef shoulder or round, in 1 chunk
1 onion

Sprinkling of freshly ground black pepper
1 tablespoon sesame oil

SAUCE

1 stalk fresh lemon grass or 1 tablespoon dried
1½ tablespoons granulated sugar
2 tablespoons shrimp sauce
1 tablespoon plus 1 teaspoon white vinegar
½ cup plus 2 tablespoons water

1 tablespoon vegetable oil
1 large clove garlic, finely chopped
1 dried hot red pepper, finely chopped, or ¼ teaspoon crushed hot pepper flakes

NOODLE PLATTER

½ pound rice sticks (*bún*) or 2½ packets of Japanese alimentary paste noodles (*somen*), cooked as directed on page 44 or 45

VEGETABLE PLATTER

1 cup fresh coriander leaves
(Chinese parsley), part of stems
attached

½ cup mint leaves

1 cup *bok choy* pieces (1½ inches
each)

1 cup bean sprouts, washed

1 cup small lettuce leaves
(preferably Boston lettuce)

1 cup fresh pineapple, sliced thin
and cut into 1-inch squares

1 cucumber, partially peeled, then
sliced in half lengthwise and
sliced across thinly

Prepare scallion brushes to decorate the meat platter first. Use only the white parts of the scallions. Cut the scallions to about 3 inches in length and remove the roots, then cut a few 1-inch-long slits in either end of each. Place the scallions in ice water and allow them to remain there until ready to use. They will curl into brushes about 30 minutes after immersion in the ice water.

Prepare the beef platter. Trim the fat off the beef, then slice paper thin and arrange in overlapping layers on a platter. Slice the onion, also paper thin, and arrange over the beef. Sprinkle black pepper over the meat and onions, then add sesame oil. Arrange the scallion brushes attractively on the platter. (This can be prepared ahead up to a few hours before serving. If so, cover with plastic wrap and refrigerate.)

If you are using fresh lemon grass, discard the outer leaves and upper two-thirds of the stalk, then chop the remainder fine. Dried lemon grass must be soaked for 2 hours and chopped fine.

Combine the sugar, shrimp sauce, vinegar, and water in a bowl. Heat the oil in a saucepan. Add the garlic and brown lightly for about 1 minute, then add the lemon grass and red pepper. Fry for another minute and add the shrimp sauce mixture. Bring to a boil and remove from the heat immediately, reserving for later use.

Arrange the vegetable platter, separating each vegetable into separate small mounds and arranging the half slices of cucumber in a circle around the outer rim.

Loosen the cooked noodles with chopsticks or your hands and arrange on a platter.

To serve, bring all the food platters to the table and transfer the shrimp sauce prepared earlier to a fondue pot; heat the sauce to bubbling. Give each diner a bowl, a pair of chopsticks, and a spoon.

Each person now selects one or two slices of beef and puts it into the bubbling sauce, together with an onion ring and a piece of *bok choy*. The meat should be cooked briefly until just pink (this will take about 30 seconds), then removed from the sauce, together with the *bok choy* and onion ring and transferred to the diner's bowl. Some noodles should then be added, a small quantity of each vegetable, a piece of pineapple, and an additional table-spoon of sauce.

This is repeated until all the food is consumed.

Rice

In Vietnam there are literally dozens of varieties of rice to choose from, each with a different texture, flavor, and its own fragrant aroma while cooking. Most Vietnamese can even tell from the aroma of the rice being cooked whether it comes from the North, Center, or South. Poorer people, who cannot afford to buy the relatively expensive, aromatic varieties, will add a few *lá dứa* leaves to the cheaper rice for their fragrant scent.

The purchase of so important a part of their diet is a serious matter to the Vietnamese. Rice is sold only by rice dealers. In general, the Vietnamese buy from a friend, someone they can trust, whose advice about which rice to buy is always sound. Bạch's mother never changed her rice dealer, nor did Bạch.

The best rice grains are long and narrow, with pointed ends, and will usually be very tender (not "mushy") when cooked. The shorter, rounder variety usually hardens when cooled. In the United States, the extra-long-grain Carolina rice is a high-quality product.

When Bạch was only ten years old, she could cook rice over a charcoal fire—quite an accomplishment, considering the difficulty most people have in preparing rice with sophisticated electric and gas stoves. The country people who manufacture and sell all their charcoal to city dwellers are even more talented. They manage to cook rice over twigs, straw, and dry leaves. Bạch's father taught her a special formula for cooking rice. The best translation is "Three times shift the pot and nine times stir the rice," meaning that when you're cooking over charcoal, you had better vary the hot spots and redistribute the rice. Of course, Bạch and most other city folks generally reserve their charcoal for barbecuing. (See page 10 for a description of the automatic rice cooker.)

We have also included in this chapter several recipes containing rice flour.

Rice with Chicken in a Clay Pot Casserole
Cơm Tay Cầm

Cooked in and served from a clay pot, this dish is very popular in all Vietnamese restaurants. Here we use a heavy, enameled iron pot. An interesting variation, the rice is prepared and served much like a pilaf, topped with the flavorsome chunks of chicken and mushrooms. It's fast, easy to prepare, and a whole meal in itself.

6 servings

CHICKEN MIXTURE

3 chicken legs with thighs
1 tablespoon thin soy sauce
2 teaspoons fish sauce (*nước mắm*)
½ teaspoon salt
1 teaspoon granulated sugar
1 teaspoon sesame oil
1 tablespoon oyster sauce
(optional)
Sprinkling of freshly ground
black pepper
3 cloves garlic, chopped

1 teaspoon vegetable oil
2 shallots or white part of 2
scallions
1 cup canned straw mushrooms
6 Chinese mushrooms, soaked for
30 minutes, then drained and
shredded
1 tablespoon cornstarch, dissolved
in ½ cup straw mushroom
water

RICE

2 cups raw extra-long-grain rice
2 tablespoons vegetable oil
2 shallots or white part of 2
scallions

3 cloves garlic, chopped
2½ cups chicken broth, fresh or
canned

Bone the chicken legs and thighs and cut the meat into bite-size pieces.

Combine the cut-up chicken with the soy sauce, fish sauce, salt, sugar, sesame oil, optional oyster sauce, black pepper, and 1 clove of the chopped garlic.

Heat the oil in a frying pan and add the chopped shallots and the remaining garlic. Add the chicken mixture and fry over medium heat until completely cooked, about 5 to 10 minutes, stirring constantly. Add the straw mushrooms and Chinese mushrooms and stir, then add the cornstarch mixture and stir again. Cook 5 minutes more, then set aside.

Rinse the rice briefly; allow it to dry for 10 minutes.

Heat the oil in a heavy, enameled iron pot and add shallots and garlic; fry until lightly browned. Add the rice and stir-fry for about 5 minutes, over high heat. Add the chicken broth. Stir at once, cover, and turn the heat down to medium. Uncover 2 times within the next 7 minutes to stir; at this point the liquid should have evaporated. Turn the heat to low and cook, covered, for an additional 10 minutes.

Place the reserved chicken on top of the rice, cover and continue cooking over low heat for 10 minutes more. Serve hot.

Mimosa Rice

Cơm Hoa Mimosa

Suffused with the warm, fascinating flavor of coconut milk, highly decorative, simulating the mimosa flower, here is a traditional main dish, served for the last course at a party.

8 servings

3 cups raw extra-long-grain rice
1 quart fresh coconut milk (see page 48) or 2 cups canned, combined with 2 cups water
1 carrot, peeled and diced
½ cup green peas, fresh or frozen
2 Chinese sausages
½ pound boneless chicken breast, diced
½ pound boneless pork loin or chops, diced
1 tablespoon fish sauce (*nước mắm*)

¼ teaspoon granulated sugar
Sprinkling of freshly ground black pepper
½ cup canned lotus seeds (optional)
5 eggs, hard boiled, shelled, and cooled
1 tablespoon vegetable oil
1 clove garlic, chopped
2 shallots or white part of 2 scallions, chopped
Sprig of fresh coriander (Chinese parsley)

Place the rice and coconut milk in a 4-quart saucepan. Bring to a boil and allow to continue boiling, uncovered, for about 3 minutes. Place a tight lid on the saucepan, immediately turn the heat to very low, and continue cooking for 20 minutes. After 20 minutes, leaving the cover on, remove the pan from the heat and allow the rice to rest for an additional 20 minutes. (The rice can remain covered for up to an hour until needed.)

While the rice is cooking, prepare the rest of the recipe. (If you wish, these additional preparations can be done several hours ahead.)

Boil the carrot in water for 5 minutes. Drain and transfer to a bowl of cold water.

Place the peas in a saucepan, cover with cold water, and bring to a boil. If you are using frozen peas, boil for about 2 minutes; if fresh, boil for 5 minutes. Drain and transfer to a bowl of cold water.

Heat a dry frying pan over medium heat. Place the sausages in the pan and brown lightly, turning occasionally, for about 5 minutes. Remove and dice.

Place the diced chicken and pork on a platter and sprinkle with the fish sauce, sugar, and black pepper. On another platter, place the carrots, peas, diced sausages, and optional lotus seeds.

Separate the cooled hard-boiled egg yolks from the whites and put both through a food mill or ricer, keeping the whites and yolks in separate mounds until the final assembling of the rice.

Heat the oil in a frying pan or wok over a high flame; add the garlic and shallots and stir briefly, being careful not to burn the garlic. Add the chicken and pork, then turn the heat down to medium and continue stirring for about 10 minutes. Add the peas, carrots, sausages, and lotus seeds and cook, stirring for about 5 minutes more to combine the ingredients well.

Uncover the rice and stir it up with chopsticks or a fork to make it fluffy. Add all the ingredients except the egg whites and yolks. Transfer the rice to a ring mold with a large center hole. Pat it firmly into the pan and then turn out onto a round platter. Sprinkle into the center all of the minced egg white and on top of it half of the egg yolk; surround the outer rim of the rice ring with the remaining egg yolk.

Put a sprig of coriander in the middle of the crown to decorate the dish and serve.

Jade Hidden in the Mountain

Ngọc Ẩn Lam Sơn

Wedding festivities in the South always include this striking dish. The multi-colored "mountain," its slopes lined with six separate ingredients, is topped by a flower inserted in the summit. An important member of the wedding party, usually a man, conveys his thanks to the guests for attending. He then removes the flower — signal for the festivities to begin.

8 servings

RICE

2 cups extra-long-grain rice
2 teaspoons vegetable oil
2 cloves garlic, chopped
2 shallots or white part of 2
   scallions, chopped
1 teaspoon tomato paste

3 cups fresh chicken broth,
   homemade or canned (1
   thirteen-ounce can with enough
   water to equal 3 cups of liquid)
½ teaspoon salt
½ teaspoon granulated sugar

CHICKEN

¾ pound boneless chicken thigh
Freshly ground black pepper
½ teaspoon granulated sugar
2 teaspoons fish sauce (*nước mắm*)

2 teaspoons vegetable oil
1 shallot or white part of 1
   scallion, chopped
2 cloves garlic, chopped

EGG PANCAKE

1 tablespoon vegetable oil

2 eggs, beaten with a sprinkling of
   black pepper and salt

VEGETABLES

1 tablespoon vegetable oil
3 cloves garlic, chopped
1 cup canned beets, cut into
   ½-inch cubes
½ green pepper, shredded

1 carrot, peeled and cut into
   ½-inch cubes
1 cup green peas, fresh or frozen
½ cup salted water

GARNISH

2 slices boiled ham, cut into thin
   strips

1 fresh flower, stemmed

Put the rice into a 4-quart pot and set aside.

Heat the oil in a saucepan; add the garlic and shallot and fry briefly, just until they become aromatic. Add the tomato paste, broth, salt, and sugar and pour over the rice.

Bring to a boil and continue to boil for about 3 minutes, then cover and turn the heat down to low. Cook for 20 minutes without uncovering. Remove from heat and set aside, without uncovering, until all the other preliminary preparations have been completed.

Cut the raw chicken into thin strips. Sprinkle with the black pepper, sugar, and fish sauce and marinate about 30 minutes. Heat the oil in a frying pan. Add the shallot and garlic and fry over high heat until slightly brown, then add the chicken. Stir well to mix and cook for about 3 minutes. Reduce the heat to medium, cover, and continue cooking for 10 minutes. Remove from the heat and set aside while you make the egg pancakes.

Heat the oil in a 10-inch frying pan. Pour in the beaten egg and rotate the pan to spread the eggs evenly. Cook on one side, then turn and cook on the other. Remove from pan, cool, and shred into thin strips. Set aside while you prepare the vegetables.

Heat 1 teaspoon of the oil in a frying pan. Add 1 clove of the chopped garlic and cook until lightly browned, then add the beets and stir-fry briefly, just long enough to coat with oil. Remove from the pan and repeat the process for the green pepper, using more of the garlic and oil, stir-frying just a little longer than the beets, which have been cooked during the canning process. Repeat the procedure for the carrot; in addition, cover and simmer for 10 minutes. Boil the green peas in the salted water for 3 minutes if using frozen peas, about 10 minutes for fresh peas. (You must retain the green color of the peas, as this symbolizes the jade, hidden in the mountain of rice.)

Have the ham strips and stemmed flower ready.

When all the components of the dish are ready, fluff up the rice with chopsticks or a fork. Immediately add the peas and mix well, making certain that the rice is completely dry. Turn the rice out onto a platter and shape into a tall peak with your hands. Decorate the slopes by distributing the following ingredients into 6 separately defined areas from top to bottom, each with its own ingredient, creating a multi-colored mountain: chicken, green pepper, beets, shredded ham, egg strips, carrot.

At this point embed the stemmed flower into the top of the mountain and serve.

Hell Rice

Cỏm Âm Phủ

This dish is magnificent from every aspect. The variety of tastes and textures is a delight to the palate, and each individual serving is a colorful display that will bring forth gasps of admiration from your party guests.

The recipe appears deceptively long only because the instructions are very precise. All of the recipe can be prepared ahead and then arranged before serving.

6 servings

BARBECUED PORK

½ pound pork butt
2 cloves garlic
2 shallots or white part of 2
   scallions

½ tablespoon fish sauce (*nước mắm*)
1½ teaspoons granulated sugar
¼ teaspoon freshly ground black pepper

Slice the pork butt paper thin. Mash all the remaining ingredients in a mortar and then combine with the sliced pork butt. Marinate for 30 minutes.

Preheat the oven to 450 degrees. Line baking pan with foil and pat the marinated pork into pan. Bake for 20 minutes on each side, then remove from the pan and cut into thin strips. Set aside.

COTTON SHRIMP

½ pound raw shrimp, shelled and
   deveined
½ teaspoon fish sauce (*nước mắm*)
Sprinkling of freshly ground
   black pepper

1 teaspoon vegetable oil
1 shallot or white part of 1
   scallion, chopped
1 clove garlic, chopped

Wash the shrimp and pat dry, then slice at an angle, against the grain. Sprinkle the fish sauce and black pepper over the shrimp.

Heat the oil in a frying pan and fry the shallot and garlic until brown. Add the shrimp, and stir until the shrimp is no longer transparent. Remove from the pan and pound in a mortar to a smooth paste. Return the shrimp to the frying pan and stir until dry. While stirring, use the back of a spoon and keep mashing until the shrimp becomes brown and very dry; the mixture should have the texture and appearance of cottony fibers that you will be able to sprinkle. Remove from the heat. (This can be done ahead and kept in the refrigerator for a few days.)

PORK CHOP

1 pork chop

Separate the meat from the pork chop bone and boil in water to cover for 15 minutes. Remove, cut into thin strips, and set aside.

EGG PANCAKE

2 eggs
Sprinkling of freshly ground
  pepper

¼ teaspoon fish sauce (*nước mắm*)
¼ teaspoon water
½ teaspoon vegetable oil

Beat the eggs with the black pepper, fish sauce, and water. Heat the oil in a 10-inch frying pan. Rotate the pan to spread the egg evenly, then cook on one side. Turn and cook on the other. Remove from the pan. Cool and cut into thin strips.

RICE

2 cups raw extra-long-grain rice

Cook the rice according to the basic recipe on page 41 and set aside.

VEGETABLES

1 cucumber
Salt
1 carrot

½ cup water
1 teaspoon granulated sugar
1 teaspoon vinegar

Cut the cucumber in half lengthwise, then slice thin crosswise. Put the slices into a bowl and sprinkle with ½ teaspoon salt. Combine well with your hands and allow to rest for 5 minutes. After 5 minutes, rinse, drain, and squeeze with your hands, removing all excess liquid. Set aside.

Cut lengthwise wedges out of the carrot, then slice thin crosswise. (Cutting the carrot this way gives it a flowerlike shape.) Put into a bowl with the water, sugar, vinegar, and a dash of salt and marinate for 30 minutes. Drain and set aside.

Arrange a plate for each person. On each one, place a mound of rice, and on the rice in wedge-shaped sections, distribute the food as follows:

A section of barbecued pork

A section of cotton shrimp

A section of pork chop

A section of shredded egg pancake

A section of cucumber

A section of Vietnamese Boiled Pâté (pages 62–64; optional)

Trim the rim of each plate with a ring of carrot flowers and place a sprig of coriander on top of the rice.

Serve with Nước Chấm (page 34).

Fried Rice with Shrimp and Crab

Cỏm Chiên Thập Cẩm

6 servings

¼ cup vegetable oil
2 shallots, chopped
¼ pound small shrimp, peeled
  and deveined
Sprinkling of salt and freshly
  ground black pepper

4 ounces crabmeat, flaked
2 eggs, lightly beaten
2 cloves garlic, chopped
4 cups cold, cooked rice
2 scallions, both white part and
  green, chopped

Heat 2 teaspoons of the oil. Add half the chopped shallots and stir, then add the shrimp, along with salt and black pepper. Fry for 3 minutes, then remove from the pan.

Heat 2 more teaspoons of the oil in the pan. Add the remaining shallots and stir, then add the crabmeat with a sprinkling of black pepper. Fry for 3 minutes, then remove and set aside.

Heat another 2 teaspoons oil in the pan. Add the eggs and cook, stirring, for 2 minutes, then remove. Heat the remaining oil. Add the garlic and stir until lightly browned, then add the rice and cook, stirring, for 7 minutes. Add the chopped scallion, stir for 3 minutes more, and return the egg, crabmeat, and shrimp to the pan. Mix well for 5 minutes.

Serve hot, with Nước Chấm (page 34).

Fried Rice with Egg

Cơm Chiên Trứng

4 servings

2 tablespoons vegetable oil
2 cloves garlic, chopped

3 cups cold, cooked rice
1 egg

Heat the oil in a frying pan. Add the garlic and cook, stirring for 1 minute, and add the rice. Stir for 7 minutes over a medium flame.

Make a well in the center of the rice, break open the egg, and drop it into the hole. Using chopsticks or a fork, stir the egg, mixing it with the rice, until all the rice is coated with egg and is yellow. Stir for a few more minutes and remove from heat.

Serve with Nước Chấm (page 34) for breakfast, lunch, or dinner.

Red Sweet or Glutinous Rice

 *Xôi Gấc*

In Vietnam, there is a red fruit with red seeds called *gấc*. The red seeds are cooked with sweet or glutinous rice, giving it a distinctive red color. More than that, the seeds impart a very special flavor and consistency to the rice, as if it were cooked with coconut milk. This dish is always served at weddings and other important occasions. *Gấc* is, of course, not available here, so we use coconut milk and a little food coloring to make a very successful copy.

8 servings

2 cups sweet or glutinous rice
3 cups coconut milk, fresh or
    canned
Few drops of red food coloring

¼ cup granulated sugar
Vietnamese Pâté, Boiled or
    Cinnamon (pages 62–64, 66)

Rinse the sweet or glutinous rice under cold water, then place in a 2-quart saucepan with the coconut milk and food coloring. Stir, then turn the heat to high and boil for 3 minutes, or until the water starts evaporating. Cover tightly, turn the heat to low, and cook for 20 minutes. Keep the pot covered until ready for the final preparations; the rice can be kept at the lowest possible heat for up to 1 hour after cooking.

When ready to serve, remove the lid, stir up the rice with chopsticks and transfer to a bowl. Mix well with the sugar and put all of the rice into a 6-inch scalloped pan. Press the rice down firmly and turn out onto a platter.

Cut the pâté into slices and arrange attractively around the rice.

NOTE

This is a party dish — usually a main course or part of a buffet. Serve at room temperature.

Puffed Glutinous Rice Balls

Xôi Chiên Phồng

Makes 4 rice balls

4 cups sweet or glutinous rice
½ cup granulated sugar

4½ cups vegetable oil

Cook the rice according to the directions on page 41, then transfer onto a large tray to cool. After it has cooled, combine with the sugar and ½ cup of the oil. Divide rice into 4 parts and shape into 4 large balls. Wrap each ball with plastic wrap and squeeze to make it very smooth. (If the balls have cracks and are not perfectly smooth, they will not puff when cooked.)

Heat the remaining oil to 375 degrees in a deep frying pan — a must for this cooking dish, as the balls of rice, if properly made, should puff up to grapefruit size. Dip a soup ladle into the oil to grease it and then, cooking only one ball at a time, follow the technique below:

Drop one rice ball into the hot oil. Immediately press down on it with the bottom of the ladle, then use the ladle to pour over some of the hot oil. Turn the ball over immediately, press, pour oil over, and turn back. This procedure must be repeated many times. The ball will puff almost immediately but it still must be pressed and the oil poured on. The more it is pressed, the more it will puff. Remove from the pan, drain, and repeat with the remaining balls.

Serve with Laqué Duck (pages 132–33).

NOTE

It's a good idea to reserve a small amount of cooked sweet or glutinous rice while you are shaping it into balls. If they crack while they are being fried, you can patch them.

Sweet Rice with Meat, Shrimp, and Sausage
Xôi Thập Cẩm

This is Bạch's creation, consisting of everything her family loves — and your family will too. Because it can be prepared ahead, it is also a convenient and substantial buffet dish.

8 to 10 servings

2 cups sweet or glutinous rice
3 cups water
⅓ cup dried shrimp
1 Chinese sausage
2 tablespoons plus 2 teaspoons vegetable oil
¼ pound boneless pork chop

3 scallions, both white and green parts
1 teaspoon fish sauce (*nước mắm*)
1 tablespoon thin soy sauce
½ teaspoon granulated sugar
Sprinkling of freshly ground black pepper

Rinse the sweet rice. Bring the water to a boil and drop in the rice. Leaving at high heat, stir once and watch the pot for about 1 minute to make certain the water doesn't boil over. When the water starts bubbling, cover the pot and remove from the heat; holding the cover tightly on the pot, drain the water into the sink. Return the pot to low heat, still covered, and cook for 20 minutes. Remove from heat, uncover, and stir up with chopsticks. (Or you can keep the rice warm for an hour over low heat and stir it up when you are ready to serve.)

Put the dried shrimp in 1 cup of cold water in a saucepan and bring to boil; cover and simmer for 30 minutes. Drain and rinse under cold water. Dice the shrimp and set aside in a bowl.

Fry the Chinese sausage in a dry frying pan until brown on all sides. Remove, dice, and add to the shrimp in the bowl.

Heat the 2 teaspoons oil in a small frying pan and fry the pork chop until brown; turn over and brown the other side. Remove from the pan and dice, then add to the shrimp and sausage.

Slice the white part of the scallions paper thin and the green part into ¼-inch pieces; arrange in separate mounds.

Heat the 2 tablespoons oil in a large frying pan or wok over high flame. Drop the scallion whites into pan and fry until brown, then add the pork, sausage, and shrimp mixture. Fry for 1 minute, stirring well, then add the scallion greens, fish sauce, soy sauce, sugar, and a sprinkling of black pepper. Continue to stir-fry for 3 minutes.

Turn the sweet rice out into a bowl and mix well with meat mixture. Transfer the contents of the bowl to a shallow, round 8-inch baking pan. Press firmly into the pan, then turn out onto a serving platter. Cut into 12 wedges.

Serve hot or cold.

NOTE

To facilitate preparation, you can prepare the meats and shrimp ahead, doing all the chopping and precooking and then assembling the dish before serving. Or, if you wish to serve it cold, you can complete the preparation several hours before serving time.

Chrysanthemum Flower Sweet Rice

 *Xôi Cúc*

Vegetarians will appreciate the versatility and nutritional balance of this breakfast dish from the North. Others will enjoy the combination of textures and tastes.

5 servings

1 cup sweet or glutinous rice
1 cup dried yellow mung beans
1 cup water
3 tablespoons vegetable oil
1 clove garlic, chopped
3 shallots or white part of 3
    scallions, thinly sliced

¼ teaspoon freshly ground black
    pepper
1 teaspoon salt
2 tablespoons cornstarch
    combined with ¼ cup water

Soak the sweet glutinous rice in water to cover overnight.

Rinse the mung beans and remove any particles that float up in the rinsing bowl, then place the mung beans in a saucepan. Add the 1 cup water and simmer over low heat for 30 minutes or until dry and tender. (To test for doneness, pick up a bean and squeeze between two fingers.) When the beans are cooked, mash them with chopsticks, a fork, or in a blender.

Heat the oil in a frying pan and add the garlic and shallots. Fry for a few seconds, then add the mashed beans, stirring well to coat with the oil. Add the black pepper and salt, mix well, and fry for about 3 minutes, stirring constantly. Transfer to a bowl and allow to cool for about 3 minutes.

Drain the rice in a colander and transfer it to a bowl; have the cornstarch-water paste ready.

Make 5 balls out of the bean mixture (see note below), using ⅓ cup of mashed beans for each ball. Roll each one in the cornstarch mixture and then in the sweet rice, pressing the rice into the bean mixture to make sure it adheres well. Press and flatten the ball almost into a thick hamburger shape. Steam (see page 30) for 30 minutes, directly on the steaming rack, or until the rice looks clear.

Serve 1 ball per person for breakfast.

NOTE

After you measure the ⅓ cup of mashed beans, press with your fingers into the cup to firm up the mixture. Then turn it out into one hand and squeeze the top with your other hand, to make it a really solid mass and easy to handle. This requires a little patience, but once you have mastered the technique you'll find it quite simple.

Happy Pancake

Bánh Khoái

A great specialty of the Center, this is indeed a happy combination of a great variety of ingredients. In Saigon, Happy Pancake, best described as a combination pancake and omelet, is served in special Center restaurants whose menu offers a variety of Center foods.

6 servings

1 cup rice flour
½ cup cornstarch
¼ cup Swansdown or other cake flour
2½ cups water
3 scallions, green part only, cut into 2-inch lengths
½ pound ground pork
2 teaspoons fish sauce (*nưóc mắm*)
2 cloves garlic, chopped
2 shallots or white part of 2 scallions, chopped

Freshly ground black pepper
½ pound shrimp, shelled and deveined, then washed and sliced in half lengthwise
½ pound bean sprouts
1 medium onion, sliced paper thin
10 fresh mushrooms, thinly sliced
3 eggs, beaten
9 tablespoons vegetable oil

Make a batter by combining the rice flour, cornstarch, cake flour, and water. Mix well and force through a sieve to eliminate lumps. Add the scallion greens to the batter and set aside.

Combine the ground pork, 1 teaspoon of the fish sauce, half the garlic, the shallots, and a sprinkle of black pepper. Add the remaining fish sauce, garlic, scallion and black pepper to the sliced shrimp.

Arrange the pork, shrimp, bean sprouts, onion, and mushrooms in separate mounds on a platter; have the batter and beaten eggs ready.

Heat a 7-inch frying pan over a high flame. Add 1 tablespoon of oil, then add 1½ tablespoons of the pork and 2 pieces of shrimp; fry until completely cooked, about 2 minutes. Reduce the heat to medium and add 3 tablespoons of batter (stirring the batter in a mixing bowl before each use), 1 tablespoon bean sprouts, a few slices of onion, and a few slices of fresh mushroom. Cover and turn the heat down to medium; cook covered, for 2 minutes, then uncover the pan and sprinkle 3 tablespoons of beaten egg over the pancake. Cover again for 2 minutes, then uncover and fold in half, omelet style. (Add ½ tablespoon more oil at this time.) Cover and cook, uncovering from time to time and turning the pancake from one side to the other to brown, always returning the cover; this should be a very crisp pancake. Repeat until all the batter and other ingredients are used up.

Serve with Basic Vegetable Platter (pages 37–38) and Nước Lèo (page 35).

Sound Pancakes

Bánh Xèo

This recipe, from the South, is a version of Happy Pancake (pages 208–9), which is made in the Center. *Xèo,* which means "sound," has two meanings — it means soft, because the pancake is not crisp like Happy Pancake, but also refers to the sound of the batter when poured into the pan. Good for do-ahead cooking, it can be kept in a warm oven for up to 3 hours.

6 servings

½ cup cornstarch
¼ cup Swansdown or other cake flour
1 cup rice flour
1 cup water
1¼ cups coconut milk, fresh or canned
¼ teaspoon turmeric
½ pound fat pork shoulder, sliced paper thin
2 cloves garlic, minced
2 teaspoons fish sauce (*nước mắm*)
2 shallots or white part of 2 scallions, minced
Freshly ground black pepper

½ pound fresh shrimp, shelled and deveined, then washed and sliced in half lengthwise
1 medium onion, sliced paper thin
½ pound bean sprouts
10 fresh mushrooms, thinly sliced
3 eggs, beaten
1 tablespoon vegetable oil for each pancake
Double recipe of Nước Chấm (see page 34)
Basic Vegetable Platter (see pages 37–38)

Make a batter by combining the cornstarch, cake flour, rice flour, water, coconut milk, and turmeric. Mix well and force through a sieve to eliminate lumps.

Combine the pork with half the garlic, 1 teaspoon of the fish sauce, half the shallots, and a sprinkling of black pepper. Combine the shrimp with the remaining fish sauce, garlic, and shallots; add a sprinkling of black pepper.

Arrange the pork, shrimp, onion slices, bean sprouts, and mushrooms on a platter in separate mounds; have the batter and beaten eggs ready.

Heat a 10-inch frying pan over high heat. Add 1 tablespoon of oil, about 4 slices of pork, a slice of shrimp and keep stirring until all are well cooked. Reduce the heat to medium and add 4½ tablespoons of batter, 1 tablespoon of bean sprouts, a few slices of onion, and a few slices of mushroom. Cover and cook for 2 minutes, then uncover, sprinkle 3 tablespoons of egg over the pancake, cover, and cook for 2 more minutes. Uncover, fold the pancake in half, as for an omelet.

Serve with *nước chấm*, and the Vegetable Platter containing lettuce, mint leaves (in season), cucumber, and fresh coriander (Chinese parsley).

Banana Leaf Cake

Bánh Lá

This is a Center dish. It can be made ahead, refrigerated, and steamed or resteamed. The cakes are usually wrapped in banana leaves and steamed, but in the West we must settle for aluminum foil — unless you have a banana tree or access to one. When they are cooked in the banana leaf, a delicate green color is imparted to the white batter. This dish is usually served with Shrimp Pâté (page 149).

8 servings

FILLING:

4 ounces raw shrimp, shelled and deveined
½ pound ground pork
2 scallions, green part only, chopped
1 tablespoon fish sauce (*nước mắm*)

¼ teaspoon freshly ground black pepper
2 teaspoons vegetable oil
2 cloves garlic, chopped
2 shallots or white part of 2 scallions, chopped

BATTER

2 cups rice flour
1 quart water

¼ teaspoon salt
¼ cup tapioca starch

Make the filling first. Cut the shrimp crosswise into thin slices. Combine with the meat and scallion greens. Sprinkle fish sauce and black pepper over meat and shrimp.

Heat the oil over a high flame; add the garlic and shallots and stir, then add the remaining ingredients. Keep stirring over high heat until completely cooked, about 5 minutes. Remove and set aside.

Combine all ingredients for the batter in a saucepan and cook over high heat, stirring constantly, until the mixture thickens. Do not stop stirring; if you do stop, the batter will not cook to the proper consistency. This takes about 5 minutes; the batter should resemble oatmeal in thickness. Remove from the heat and keep stirring for about 2 more minutes, until the mixture becomes smooth.

To form cakes, cut 2 dozen pieces aluminum foil into 6 × 10-inch rectangles. Take 1½ tablespoons of the batter and spread it over one of the

Figure 5

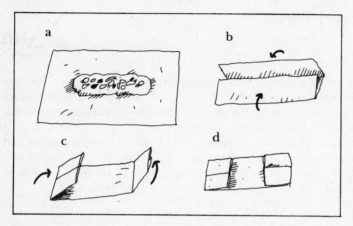

pieces of aluminum foil, measuring about 4 × 6 inches. Spread 1 tablespoon of the prepared filling over the batter, pressing it in slightly. Fold the foil over to enclose the package, the wide ends first, one overlapping the other (fig. 5). Turn the package over and fold the narrow ends over to enclose the sides. The folds of the foil should be along the edges of the paste. This will make a very neat, compact package. Continue until all the ingredients are used up.

Place all the packages on the rack of a metal steamer and steam, covered, for 30 minutes (see page 30). Allow to cool before serving.

Serve with Nước Chấm (page 34).

NOTE

If the cakes are completely cooked, they will be transparent. If there are any white areas, the package should be resealed and returned to the steamer. These cakes can be frozen and re-steamed later, or just kept in the refrigerator for a few days.

Rolling Cake

Bánh Cuốn

Rolling Cake is not a dessert, but a charming literal translation from the Vietnamese. It is really like a fresh rice-paper roll, except that it is folded. This dish can be prepared several hours ahead and then steamed or served at room temperature.

After you make a few fresh rice papers, you will become quite adept and will find it both time saving and easy to place the filling on each paper as it comes from the pan. However, at first you might want to prepare the filling, set it aside, then make the rice papers and finally assemble them.

8 servings

ROLLING CAKES

10 tree ears
4 black Chinese mushrooms
¾ pound ground pork
1 teaspoon fish sauce (*nước mắm*)
¼ teaspoon freshly ground black
    pepper

1 teaspoon oil
2 shallots or white part of 2
    scallions, chopped
2 cloves garlic, chopped
¼ cup chopped onion
Fresh Rice Papers (page 43)

ACCOMPANIMENTS FOR SERVING

2 tablespoons vegetable oil
2 tablespoons dried onion flakes
  (see note page 215)
1 cup bean sprouts, blanched for
  ½ minute in boiling water
1 cucumber, shredded

¼ cup chopped mint leaves
¼ cup chopped fresh coriander
  (Chinese parsley)
Vietnamese Pâté (pages 62–66;
  optional)
Nước Chấm (page 34)

In separate bowls, soak the tree ears and mushrooms in warm water for 30 minutes. Drain, chop fine, and set aside.

Combine the pork with the fish sauce and black pepper.

Heat the oil and add the shallots and garlic and fry for a few seconds, then add the onion. Add the meat mixture to the pan and fry until all trace of red color is gone. Add the finely chopped mushrooms and tree ears; fry for a few more minutes. Remove the filling from the pan and reserve for later use.

Prepare the fresh rice papers as in the basic recipe. As each rice paper comes from the pan, drop it onto an oiled cookie sheet and place 1 teaspoon of filling in the center of the pancake horizontally, leaving equal space on each side. Fold both sides over the meat first, then the top part. Fill all the pancakes and set aside.

Heat the 2 tablespoons oil in a small saucepan on a high flame and fry the dried onion for 2 seconds or until lightly browned. Remove at once.

To serve, give each person an individual plate already arranged with 6 filled pancakes. Garnish them with a sprinkle of dried onion, 2 tablespoons of bean sprouts, about 2 tablespoons cucumber, sprinkling of *nước chấm*, 1 teaspoon coriander, 1 teaspoon chopped mint leaves, and a few slices of the pâté.

NOTE

Dried onions are available, flaked, in the spice department of supermarkets. In Vietnam we always fry shallots in oil, after slicing and drying for several hours, but we find the dried onion gives a similar flavor with much less work.

Glutinous Rice Cakes

Bánh Dày

Wherever people from Northern Vietnam settle, you will find a store where these cakes are prepared. For breakfast, Bach would go out early in the morning and bring these home on a banana leaf, on which they would be served.

They are served with a Vietnamese pâté, which you can make at home (see pages 61–66) or purchase in a Vietnamese grocery, if you are fortunate enough to live near one.

Makes 3 dozen cakes

1 pound sweet or glutinous rice flour	1 teaspoon salt
	1 cup boiling water

Place the flour and salt in a large bowl, reserving ¼ cup of the flour for dusting your hands. Add the boiling water a little at a time, combining with chopsticks after each addition. After all the water has been added, wait about 30 seconds and then knead for about 5 minutes, until the dough becomes elastic.

Dip your fingers in the reserved flour. Break off a piece of dough, about 1 heaping tablespoonful. Shape into a ball and flatten slightly.

Bring water to a boil in the bottom of a steamer. Place the cakes on aluminum foil on steamer rack, leaving some holes uncovered so that wet steam can circulate freely. Cover and steam for 15 minutes, then remove.

Serve as a snack or for breakfast, with Vietnamese pâté.

NOTE

The cakes can be made ahead of time and kept refrigerated or frozen. They can be reheated in the steamer or at room temperature. Our favorite brand of sweet rice flour is Tienley; our second choice is Mochiko, both available in Oriental markets.

Noodles and Noodle Soups

In Vietnam it is never necessary for anyone to prepare noodles at home. They are prepared fresh daily and sold in the market, ready to eat. They are simply brought home and combined with the dish being cooked. There are many kinds of noodles. some used only for a specific dish. For example, the noodles called *bánh phở* are used only for Hanoi Soup.

In the West, we have had some difficulty in reproducing these dishes, but with a great deal of experimentation we have worked out more than satisfactory substitutes, using Japanese and Chinese dried noodles. In most cases it is impossible to distinguish them from the original Vietnamese noodle.

Noodles are either heated by the broth or food with which they are eaten, or are served at room temperature, as are many Vietnamese dishes.

In each recipe where we use noodles, we will always specify which kind to use. We are this specific because so many different noodles are labeled confusingly, and sometimes the labels are downright misleading.

Hue Beef Noodle Soup with Lemon Grass
Bún Bò Huế

Hue is the ancient capital of central Vietnam, where Bạch's mother was born. In the Center, the tomato paste is generally fried with powdered hot chili peppers before being added to the soup. Prepared this way, the soup, served both piping and spicy hot, will almost surely bring tears to your eyes. Bach prefers not to prepare it with the chili peppers — "too strong for the children." You can make your own decision as to just how you want to serve it.

This soup is served as an entire meal.

6 servings

2 stalks fresh lemon grass or 2 tablespoons dried
9 cups cold water
1½ pounds boneless beef shank, cut into 1-inch slices
1 pound fresh pork hocks, cut through the bone, into 1-inch slices
3 tablespoons fish sauce (*nước mắm*)
1 teaspoon salt
Dash of MSG (optional)
1 teaspoon vegetable oil
1 tablespoon tomato paste

1 teaspoon shrimp sauce, mixed well with 1 teaspoon water
½ pound rice sticks (*bún*) or 2½ packets Japanese alimentary paste noodles (*somen*), cooked according to the directions on page 44 or 45
1 small onion, thinly sliced
2 tablespoons mixed chopped fresh coriander (Chinese parsley) and scallion green
1 cup shredded cucumber
1 cup shredded lettuce

If using fresh lemon grass, discard the outer leaves and upper two-thirds of the stalk and simply cut the remainder crosswise into 3-inch sections.

Bring the water to a boil and drop in the beef shank, lemon grass, and pork hocks. Boil, uncovered, for 15 minutes, removing scum from the top 3 times during that period. Turn the heat down to medium, cover, and simmer for 1½ hours. (If after 1 hour of cooking the hock is tender, remove from the pot and set aside while the shin beef continues cooking.) When the beef is tender, remove it from the pot and add to the broth, the fish sauce, salt, and optional MSG.

Heat the oil in a small frying pan; add the tomato paste and fry for about 1 minute, then pour into the soup. (The purpose of frying the tomato paste is to make it float on top of the soup; if you omit this step, the paste will not float.) Add the shrimp sauce mixture and boil for another 5 minutes.

After the meat has cooled, cut it into thin slices; cut each pork hock slice into 2 chunks.

Serve in individual soup bowls. Place the noodles on the bottom of each, then the two kinds of meat, then some onion rings. Sprinkle on the coriander and scallion and pour the hot soup over everything. (If you want more salt, add plain fish sauce.) Then add about 2 tablespoons of shredded cucumber and 2 tablespoons of shredded lettuce to each bowl and serve.

Saigon Soup

Hủ Tiếu

There are special "breakfast" restaurants serving Saigon Soup, just as there are for Hanoi Soup. Unusual for Westerners, Saigon Soup may be served with the dry ingredients in one bowl and the broth in another. When I first tried Saigon Soup in a Vietnamese restaurant in Paris, I was intrigued by the words *avec ou sans bouillon* ("with or without broth"). Curious, I ordered it without broth and was delighted with it, even without the broth. The assortment of ingredients in this dish is enough to gladden the heart of any food lover or adventurous eater.

6 servings

2 chicken thighs
6 ounces pork butt
6 ounces beef round
Sprinkling of freshly ground
  black pepper
2 tablespoons fish sauce (*nước mắm*)
6 large shrimp, peeled, deveined, and cut in half lengthwise
½ pound crabmeat, fresh, frozen, or canned
1 stalk celery
6 sprigs watercress
1 quart homemade chicken stock or 1 (13¾ ounces) can chicken broth plus 2 cans of water

½ teaspoon salt
1 veal or pork heart
2 teaspoons preserved vegetable
5 tablespoons vegetable oil
1 clove garlic, chopped
2 shallots or white part of 2 scallions, chopped
5 shallots, sliced thinly
1 pound dried *sha-wo-fun* noodles or rice sticks (*bánh phở*)
3 tablespoons chopped Roasted Peanuts (page 46)
Nước Chấm (page 34; optional)

Bone the chicken thighs and cut the meat into 1-inch cubes. Slice the pork thin, then cut into 1 × 2-inch squares. Slice the beef and cut into squares the same size as the pork. Sprinkle the black pepper and 1 tablespoon of the fish sauce over the meats, shrimp, and crab.

Slice the celery thin, on the slant; cut the watercress into 3 crosswise sections. Set aside.

Put the chicken stock and/or broth water into a large pot. Add the remaining 1 tablespoon fish sauce, the salt, and the veal heart to the cold liquid. Bring to a boil, then add the preserved vegetable, cover, and boil for 15 min-

utes. Turn off flame. Remove the heart from broth and cut in half lengthwise, then into lengthwise slices; set aside.

Heat 2 tablespoons of the oil over a high flame. Add the chopped garlic and half the chopped shallot; stir for a few seconds, then add the crabmeat and fry until lightly browned. Remove from the pan and set aside.

Heat another 2 tablespoons of the oil. Add the rest of the chopped shallot, then the pork and chicken; stir until the pork looks white and the chicken no longer looks translucent. Cover, turn the flame down to medium, and cook for 10 minutes. Uncover the pan, add the beef and shrimp and stir-fry until completely cooked, about 5 minutes longer. Set aside.

Heat the remaining 1 tablespoon of oil, add the sliced shallots, and fry over high heat until brown. Remove and set aside.

Boil the noodles as directed on page 44.

Arrange the soup in 6 individual bowls as follows: Fill half of each bowl with noodles, then put some of each of the meats on top of the noodles. Sprinkle the crabmeat and fried shallots over the meats and place a few pieces of watercress and a few pieces of celery on top. Sprinkle about 1 teaspoon roasted peanuts in each bowl, then pour the broth over everything and sprinkle on a little *nước chấm*, if desired.

NOTE

As we mentioned before, the broth can be served in a separate bowl.
Dried sha-wo-fun noodles are available in Oriental grocery stores.

Chicken and Rice Noodles with Pork and Egg
Bún Thang

Ba Ba Bung is a popular restaurant in Saigon, always crowded in the mornings with students and housewives. The restaurant's name is an apt description of the owner — *Ba Ba*, meaning "third-born," and *Bung*, meaning "special belly"; the word picture is complete. A typically substantial northern breakfast, *bún thang* can also be served as a very satisfying single-dish family meal.

6 servings

2½ quarts water
1 pound chicken legs with thighs
1½ pound chicken necks and
  backs
6 ounces pork loin
4 teaspoons fish sauce (*nước mắm*)
Salt
2 eggs, beaten
Sprinkling of freshly ground
  black pepper

1 teaspoon vegetable oil
½ pound rice sticks (*bún*) or 2½
  packets Japanese alimentary
  paste noodles (*somen*)
Vietnamese Boiled Pâté (pages
  62–64; optional)
1 small onion, sliced paper thin
1 tablespoon mixed chopped
  fresh coriander (Chinese
  parsley) and scallion green
Shrimp sauce (optional)

Bring to a boil the 2½ quarts of water, together with the chicken legs, necks, and backs and the pork. Turn the heat down to medium and simmer, uncovered, for 20 minutes. Remove the chicken legs and continue to boil the necks and backs and the pork for another 10 minutes. Remove the pork and continue to cook the necks and backs for another 10 minutes in order to enrich the broth; remove the necks and backs, then add the fish sauce and 1 teaspoon salt.

While the broth is cooking, make the following additional preparations: Remove the chicken meat from the bones and shred; shred the pork.

Beat the eggs and add salt and black pepper. Heat the oil in an 8-inch frying pan; make a pancake of the eggs as directed on page 208. Remove from the pan, cool, and shred into thin strips.

Prepare the noodles according to the directions on page 44 or 45.

To serve, arrange individual soup bowls as follows:

Fill two-thirds of each bowl with noodles. Put some shredded chicken, pork, pancake strips, and Vietnamese pâté into separate segments on top of the noodles in such a way that each is distinguishable. Then add a few onion slices and some coriander and scallion green and pour hot broth over all.

Stir about ½ teaspoon shrimp sauce into each soup bowl, if desired, and serve.

Chicken Noodle Soup with Dried Bamboo Shoots

Bún Măng

In Vietnam, dried bamboo shoots lend their subtle flavor and unusual texture to many soup recipes. This one is a particular favorite.

6 servings

1 cup dried bamboo shoots
½ pound rice sticks (*bún*) or 2½ packets Japanese alimentary paste noodles (*somen*)
2½ quarts homemade chicken broth or 2 cans (13¾ ounces) chicken broth plus 1½ quarts water
2 chicken legs with thighs

½ cup sliced canned bamboo shoots
1 tablespoon plus 1 teaspoon fish sauce (*nước mắm*)
1 teaspoon salt
1 tablespoon mixed minced fresh coriander (Chinese parsley) and scallion green

🔥 Cover the dried bamboo shoots with water in a saucepan and bring to a boil. Boil for 30 minutes and drain, then boil again in 1 quart of water for 2 hours. Drain and shred coarsely. Set aside.

Cook the noodles according to the directions on page 44 or 45.

Pour chicken broth into a large pot. Drop the chicken legs and thighs into the cold liquid and heat to a boil; cook for 30 minutes. Remove the chicken from the pot, and then add the precooked bamboo shoots, canned bamboo shoots, fish sauce, and salt. Turn the heat down to a simmer and cook for 30 minutes.

To serve, arrange some shredded chicken, noodles, and both varieties of bamboo shoots in each soup bowl. Pour the broth over all and sprinkle minced coriander and scallions on top.

Chicken Cellophane Noodle Soup
Miến Gà

The contrasting textures of the chewy giblets, the resilient cellophane noodles, and the tangy seasoning make this fast and easy-to-prepare soup a good addition to your list of dishes that please everyone.

6 servings

4 ounces cellophane noodles
2 quarts water
1 pound chicken necks, skin removed (see note below)
2 chicken legs with thighs
½ pound chicken giblets
3 tablespoons fish sauce (*nước mắm*)

½ teaspoon salt
Dash of MSG (optional)
Freshly ground black pepper
2 tablespoons mixed chopped fresh coriander (Chinese parsley) and scallion green

Soak the cellophane noodles in warm water for 10 minutes, then drain and cut into 3-inch lengths.

Bring the 2 quarts water to a boil and drop in the chicken necks, legs, and giblets. Boil for 7 minutes, then remove giblets; slice and reserve them for use later. Continue cooking the broth for another 15 minutes, then strain, discarding the necks. Remove and shred all meat from legs and thighs. Add the fish sauce, salt, and a dash of MSG to the broth; sprinkle with black pepper. Just before serving, bring the soup to a boil and add the cellophane noodles.

To serve, remove the noodles from the soup and use to fill individual bowls half full. Sprinkle on some shredded chicken, giblets, and chopped scallion, and coriander. Pour boiling broth over all, sprinkle on some black pepper, and serve.

NOTE

Reserve the skin for Stuffed Chicken Necks Cooked in Coconut Milk (page 89).

Shrimp Crab Meatball Noodle Soup

Bún Tôm Cua Thịt Nạc

6 servings

½ pound rice sticks (*bún*) or 2½ packets Japanese alimentary paste noodles (*somen*)

½ pound raw shrimp, shelled and deveined

6 ounces ground pork

2 cloves garlic, chopped

2 shallots or white part of 2 scallions, chopped

1½ teaspoons salt

2 tablespoons plus 1½ teaspoons fish sauce (*nước mắm*)

½ teaspoon freshly ground black pepper

½ teaspoon granulated sugar

1 can (7 ounces) crabmeat

6 cups water

2 tablespoons mixed chopped fresh coriander (Chinese parsley) and scallion green

Cook the noodles according to the instructions on page 44 or 45.

In a mortar, blender, or food processor, mash the shrimp slightly, then add the ground pork and blend to a smooth paste. Transfer to a large bowl and add the garlic, shallots, ½ teaspoon of the salt, 1½ teaspoons fish sauce, black pepper, and sugar.

Drain the water from the can of crabmeat and add one-quarter of the crabmeat at a time to the meat-shrimp mixture, pounding it in with a pestle (don't use the blender or food processor for this step).

Shape the meat-seafood mixture into 36 balls, first dipping your hands in oil.

In a large pot, bring 6 cups of water to a boil and drop the balls into it. While the water is boiling, add the 2 tablespoons fish sauce and 1 teaspoon salt. Boil for 10 minutes.

To serve, fill individual bowls half full of noodles. Place 6 balls on top and add the broth. Sprinkle with chopped coriander and scallions and serve.

Fresh Rice Noodles Fried with Assorted Meats

Bánh Phở Xaò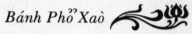

Fresh rice noodles are simply a thicker fresh rice paper that you can prepare yourself (see the recipe for Fresh Rice Papers on page 43, using 3 tablespoons batter per rice paper instead of 2 tablespoons). Also known to Chinese cooks as *sha-wo-fun*, these are obtainable in many Oriental groceries in the Chinatown areas of larger cities. However, our recipe is so simple that you should not deprive yourself of this because of the possible unavailability of *sha-wo-fun*. Fresh rice papers or *sha-wo-fun* can be refrigerated or frozen and resteamed when needed; you may also use rice sticks (*bánh phở*).

Stir-fried dishes are generally served as part of a meal. This substantial dish is unusual in that it is a whole meal in itself. We think it will become a "standard" in your repertoire.

6 servings

1 chicken thigh
2 ounces lean beef
4 ounces pork or beef liver
2 ounces lean pork
2 large shrimp, shelled and deveined
1 small onion
4 stalks *bok choy*
2 scallions, both white and green parts
Freshly ground black pepper
3½ teaspoons fish sauce (*nước mắm*)

1 teaspoon cornstarch
1 teaspoon granulated sugar
1 teaspoon oyster sauce
½ cup water
3 tablespoons vegetable oil
4 cloves garlic, crushed and chopped
Fresh Rice Papers (page 43), prepared with 3 tablespoons batter per 6 servings rice paper and cut into ½-inch-thick slices, or *sha-wo-fun* (see note above)

Bone the chicken and cut the meat into ½-inch cubes. Slice the beef and liver paper thin; slice the lean pork paper thin and then into ½-inch pieces. Slice the shrimp into thin crosswise pieces.

Cut the onion into lengthwise quarters and separate the segments. Cut the *bok choy* horizontally into 1-inch pieces; separate the white part from the green. Cut the scallions into 2-inch lengths.

Arrange all vegetables and meats on a large platter to facilitate final cooking, sprinkling black pepper and 1½ teaspoons of the fish sauce on the shrimp and meat.

In a bowl, combine the 2 teaspoons fish sauce, the cornstarch, sugar, oyster sauce, and water. Heat a frying pan over a high flame; add 2 tablespoons of the oil and half the garlic. Drop in the noodles and fry very quickly, just long enough to coat them with oil and absorb the garlic flavor. Remove from the pan and spread on a large platter.

Heat the remaining 1 tablespoon oil. Add the remaining garlic cloves and fry, then add the chicken and pork, and fry, stirring constantly, for 3 minutes. Add the beef, scallions, liver, and white part of the *bok choy*. Keep stirring until the beef is still slightly pink, then add the green part of the *bok choy*, and stir for an additional 2 minutes. Add the combined cornstarch mixture and stir until the sauce thickens slightly. Pour over the noodles, sprinkle with black pepper and serve hot.

Desserts

The traditional Vietnamese dessert consists of any of the many kinds of fruit that are always available. When a prepared dessert is served, it is really a reflection of the French influence and is frequently a Western-style dessert. We have included in this chapter some Vietnamese desserts that tend to be a bit sweet, with interesting variations in texture.

"Cigarette" Cookies

Bánh Sen Tán

Yields 100 cookies

1 pound dried yellow mung
  beans, without husks
4½ cups water
4 cups granulated sugar

3½ cups all-purpose flour
4 cups coconut milk, fresh or
  canned

Wash the mung beans and rinse many times, removing all small stones, green husks, and so on. It can take about 10 minutes to get them really clean. Bring the water to a boil in a large saucepan; drop in the mung beans. Cover and simmer until tender, about 20 minutes. Pour the water and beans into a blender and blend until smooth. Transfer to a large bowl.

Combine the sugar with the flour and coconut milk in a blender or food processor and blend until smooth. Add this to the mung bean mixture.

Heat a no-stick frying pan, approximately 8 to 10 inches in diameter, over a low flame. Dip a brush into the batter and lightly paint a 5-inch square in the center of the pan. You will probably have to make about 3 strokes in each direction to fill in the square. (It is desirable to have as thin a cookie as possible — a little practice will develop your technique.) Cook for about 5 minutes, or until the cookie becomes quite brown. Place a 5½-inch-long wooden dowel or stiff paper cylinder on one edge of the cookie while it is still in the pan and roll it cigarette fashion. Remove the cookie from the cylinder right away, as it will harden immediately.

Continue in this fashion until all the batter is used.

NOTE

These can be stored in a tin box, jar, or plastic bag for several months.

Steamed Rice Coconut Milk Cake

Bánh Bò Nước Dừa Hấp

20 servings

1 pound rice flour
3 cups coconut milk
1 teaspoon active dry yeast
1 wine rice ball, crushed to a
  powder

3 cups granulated sugar
1 teaspoon lemon juice
1 teaspoon water

Combine 3 tablespoons of the rice flour, ¼ cup of the coconut milk, and ½ teaspoon of yeast with the wine rice ball. Cover and allow to stand at room temperature for 3 hours.

Cook 2½ cups of the coconut milk with the sugar just long enough to melt the sugar. Remove from the heat and cool.

After the yeast-rice flour mixture has rested for 3 hours, combine it with the coconut milk-sugar mixture. Mix well, cover, and allow it to rest at room temperature for another 3 hours. At the end of the resting time, combine the mixture with the remaining coconut milk, the lemon juice, and the remaining ½ teaspoon of yeast, which should first be dissolved in the teaspoon of water. Transfer to several small bowls or pans so that the mixture fills it only halfway, to allow room for expansion. Let stand overnight, at room temperature. The following day, steam (using the wet steaming method as described on page 36) for 30 minutes.

Serve the cake either hot, cold, or at room temperature.

NOTE

A wine rice ball can be purchased in Oriental grocery stores. They are about the size of a camphor ball, and white. To crush, use a rolling pin or a blender.

Bean Curd Dessert

 *Đậu Hủ*

6 servings

1 cup dried soybeans
3 quarts water
4 ounces rice flour

2 teaspoons gypsum powder
1 tablespoon hot water

SYRUP

1 pound brown sugar
2 cups water

1 one-inch piece fresh gingerroot,
  shredded
Lime juice

Soak the soybeans overnight, or for at least 3 hours. Drain. Transfer the soaked beans and add the 3 quarts water, part of each at a time, to a blender and blend until smooth. After all the soybeans and water have been blended, pour the milk into either a cheesecloth bag or a linen dish towel and squeeze all the liquid into a bowl through a mesh strainer. Discard the pulp.

Put the rice flour in a small bowl. Add ½ cup of the soybean milk, stir well, and set aside.

Put the gypsum powder into a small custard cup.

To successfully prepare this dessert, which is a form of bean curd, the following instructions should be followed carefully:

Set on a counter a large, clean pot with a tight cover. Place the small cup containing the gypsum powder next to it.

Bring the 2 bowls of soybean milk to the stove. Pour the milk (without the rice flour) into a pot large enough so the milk will not pour over the sides when it boils. Set the pot on a burner and turn the heat to high. Wait until steam is rising from the pot before inserting a spoon to stir. When the steam does appear, stir the milk clockwise (to the right) and never change the direction in which you stir. When the bean milk appears foamy (after about 3 minutes), add the bean milk-rice flour mixture, continuing to stir.

At this point — not sooner — add the 1 tablespoon of hot water to the gypsum powder. Turn the heat to very low, and then, working quickly to prevent failure, paint the inside bottom and sides of the large, clean pot with gypsum paste. Immediately pour the boiling soybean milk into the pot and cover with a tight lid. In 20 minutes this will jell or become solid.

Make a syrup by combining the sugar and 2 cups water in a saucepan. Bring to a boil, add the ginger to the boiling liquid, and remove from the heat immediately.

To serve, remove the bean curd from the pot by slicing layers across the top with a spatula, rather than by scooping it out with a spoon.

Place these slices into individual bowls and pour 2 tablespoons of syrup over each serving. Add a squeeze of lime juice and serve warm or cold.

Banana Sweet Soup
Chè Chuối

8 servings

1 cup granulated sugar
6 whole ripe bananas, peeled
2½ cups coconut milk, canned or
  fresh
½ cup water
½ cup arrowroot vermicelli,
  soaked in cold water for 15
  minutes and drained

¼ cup pearl tapioca, rinsed in
  cold water and drained
¼ cup Toasted Sesame Seeds
  (page 46)

Sprinkle the sugar over the bananas and allow to stand for 30 minutes. Combine the sugared bananas, coconut milk, and water in a saucepan. Cover and simmer for 15 minutes. Add the arrowroot vermicelli and tapioca and cook, covered, for an additional 7 to 10 minutes, until the tapioca pearls are clear and translucent.

Remove from the heat and, if you wish to serve it hot (it can be refrigerated and served cold), put into individual dessert bowls. Before serving, hot or cold, sprinkle about ½ teaspoon of toasted sesame seeds on each portion.

NOTE

Arrowroot vermicelli can be purchased in Oriental markets.

Menu Planning

The great variety of flavors, textures, and colors found in Vietnamese dishes provide an endless range of possibilities in preparing meals, whether they be simple family dinners or the much more elaborate repasts for special occasions.

Balance is crucial. Try to present as many different tastes, textures, and colors as possible. The order in which the dishes are served should be from delicate on to the more highly flavored or spicy ones. The menus in our lists are designed to help, but don't hesitate to experiment on your own. Because desserts are not typically part of a Vietnamese meal, we have not included them in the menu. Serve any Western dessert you wish or pick one from the chapter on desserts. Of course, you can also follow Vietnamese tradition and serve fruit.

The Place Setting

The place setting consists of the following:

Everything is served in bowls. The bowl used for rice and soup is similar in shape to a cup (but without ears), about 5 to 6 inches across. For whole-meal soups, a bowl twice as large is used.

The bowls rest on a flat plate, 6 to 8 inches in diameter. This plate simply serves to hold discarded bones, shells, and so forth. Chopsticks are made of bamboo, ebony, and ivory, among other materials. Bamboo is most popular and is generally used for family dinners; the more expensive chopsticks are used for party dinners. Chopsticks are placed to the right of the plate, on top of the napkin. Chopstick rests are optional. The soup spoon is usually of metal (generally stainless steel, which is more popular than silver) and is placed to the left of the plate.

Dipping dishes — small shallow saucers or bowls about 3 inches in diameter — are placed on the right at the top of the plate. There may be two, three, or more, depending on the elaborateness of the meal.

The Family Dinner

The family dinner very often consists of a soup, a simmered main dish, and a stir-fried dish, all placed on the table at one time. There is no special order in which they are eaten.

Each diner is given a bowl of rice. He helps himself to a small amount of food from the serving dish and places it on top of the rice in his bowl. On the way to the rice bowl, he may dip it in a sauce or do so afterwards. The soup is served over the rice in the bowl. Each diner eats whatever he likes and refills his rice bowl until he is satisfied. (Bach's husband is a "three bowls of rice" man. Gloria's husband has only recently risen to such heights!)

Each of the family dinners in this section serves 6 and are all served with rice.

The Party Dinner

The food served at parties or special occasions is much more elaborate in appearance, as well as in the intricacy of the recipes and the number of dishes served. The amount of preparation going into a dinner for friends is an important indication of the respect and regard in which they are held.

Rice is never served plain, but is specially prepared with extra ingredients for more flavor and color. Soups are much more complicated and are prepared with expensive ingredients. They are not served over rice, as in the family dinner.

When the guests arrive, they are first served tea in the living room. After tea, they move into the dining room. Appetizers — at least one, usually two — are served first with drinks — usually wine for the men and soft drinks for the ladies. The soup is served next, followed by the main dishes and a highly decorative rice dish. Dessert is, more often than not, some fruit. After dinner, the guests move back to the living room for tea.

Each of the party menus in this chapter will serve 8 to 10 diners. Incidentally, those who worry about stir-frying or other last-minute preparation can relax. These menus can be prepared ahead.

Tea

 *Trà*

In Vietnam, as one might expect, tea is the universal beverage. On awakening in the morning, one prepares tea immediately, not only for breakfast, but for the entire day. During the day, it is kept in a padded tea cozy. Friends drop in unannounced, as is the custom, and the host must be ready to serve tea on their arrival. Tea is served before and after meals, never during meals.

Vietnam grows its own tea on plantations in the cool highlands of the Center. The tea plantation area, which is in the province of Dalat, is called Blao; the most popular tea in Vietnam is "Blao" tea. The Vietnamese are very fond of tea mixed with dried flowers — roses, jasmine, chrysanthemums, and lotus blossoms. Tea with dried lotus blossoms is the favorite.

Poetry, tea, and snacks go together in Vietnamese hospitality. Traditionally, after work or on weekends, friends were invited in for tea, snacks, and poetry. Each guest, after finishing his cup of tea, was required to compose a poem, the participants vying with each other to create the best poem. The tea was served strong in very small teapots, each holding about one cup, and with tiny cups about 1 inch in diameter and 2 inches deep.

Family Menus

1

Fried Chicken with Lemon Grass and Red Pepper (page 129)
Soup with Cabbage Pork Rolls (page 170)
Fried Fish with Fresh Tomato Sauce (page 145)

2

Steamed Fish (pages 142–43)
Three-Meat Vegetable Dish (page 116)
Beef Soup with Pineapple and Tomato (page 175)

3

Steamed Egg and Mushrooms (page 139)
Pork Cooked with Coconut Water (page 106)
Soup with Bok Choy and Cellophane Noodles (page 179)

4
Simmered Fish (page 148)
Beef Soup with Lemon Grass (page 176)
Fried Chicken with Broccoli (page 130)

5
Stuffed Squash Soup (pages 171–72)
Simmered Chicken with Ginger (page 126)
Bean Sprouts Fried with Shrimp and Pork (page 115)

6
Tomatoes Stuffed with Ground Pork (pages 111–12)
Taro Soup with Ground Pork (page 173)
Cauliflower with Straw Mushrooms (page 165)

7
Chicken Soup with Lily Buds and Cellophane Noodles (page 178)
Pork Simmered with Five Spice Powder (page 108)
Stir-Fried Beef with Green Peppers and Broccoli (page 98)

8
Beef and French-Fried Potatoes (page 100)
Papaya Soup with Pork Hock (page 174)
Pork and Shrimp Simmered with Fish Sauce (page 114)

Party Menus

1
Cabbage with Meat in the Shape of a Clock (pages 74–75)
Spring Rolls (pages 58–60)
Chicken Cellophane Noodle Soup (page 225)
Rice with Chicken in a Clay Pot Casserole (pages 192–93)

2
Cabbage with Meat and Dried Jellyfish (page 77)
Meat-Stuffed Squid (pages 78–79)
Shaking Beef (page 96)
Asparagus Crab Soup (page 182)
Jade Hidden in the Mountain (pages 196–97)

3

Vegetables with Meat in a Grapefruit Shell (page 76)
Vietnamese Roast Beef with Ginger Sauce (page 95)
Boneless Stuffed Whole Fish (page 144)
Barbecued Pork with Rice Noodles (pages 104–5)

4

Bamboo Shoots with Shrimp and Meat (page 81)
Banana Leaf Cake (pages 212–13)
Shrimp Pâté (page 149)
Hue Beef Noodle Soup with Lemon Grass (pages 218–19)

5

Barbecued Beef Wrapped in Fresh Rice Papers (pages 92–93)
Happy Pancake (pages 208–9)
Shrimp Crab Meatball Noodle Soup (page 226)
Hell Rice (pages 198–200)

6

Crab Fried with Salt (page 83)
Beef, Shrimp, and Fish Fondue with Coconut Water (pages 186–87)
Mimosa Rice (pages 194–95)
Dried Jellyfish with Cucumber (page 80)

7

Vietnamese Boneless Stuffed Chicken (pages 122–23)
Lettuce Roll with Shrimp, Meat, and Noodle (page 82)
Barbecued Meatballs (page 69)

8

Shredded Chicken with Small Mint Leaves (page 128)
Shrimp Cakes (page 150)
Creamed-Corn Chicken Soup (page 180)
Shrimp on Sugar Cane (pages 67–68)

Shopping List and Mail Order Suppliers

If you keep the following ingredients in your pantry, you will always be able to prepare Vietnamese food, with additions from your local market.

_____ Long-grain rice

_____ Sweet (glutinous) rice

_____ Rice sticks (*banh pho*)

_____ Rice sticks (*bun*)

_____ Tiny rice noodles (*banh hoi*)

_____ Dried rice papers (*banh trang*)

_____ Bottled fish sauce

_____ Lemon grass

_____ Cellophane noodles

_____ Tree ears

_____ Lily buds

_____ Peanuts with red inner skins

_____ Raw sesame seeds

_____ Canned coconut milk

_____ Tuong

_____ Shrimp sauce

_____ Bamboo shoots (canned)

_____ Bamboo shoots (dried)

_____ Preserved vegetable

_____ Five spice powder

_____ Star anise

_____ Vegetable oil

_____ Oriental sesame seed oil

_____ Thin soy sauce

_____ Tomato paste

_____ White vinegar

_____ Straw mushrooms
_____ garlic
_____ shallots
_____ Oriental dried mushrooms

If you do not have a Vietnamese or other Oriental store in your immediate area we have included a listing of such stores throughout the country. We believe that all of them will fill mail orders, however, you might write or telephone first. We know that Vietnam House, in Connecticut, Xuan Thu in Texas, and Mekong Center in Virginia will fill mail orders; we shop there and they have agreed to coordinate any mail orders with our shopping list. When you send them your order, they will send you a bill and, upon receipt of your check, they will mail the ingredients to you anywhere in the United States.

Viet Nam Thuc Phan
Menlo Park, CA 94025

A Dong Thuc Pham
6001 Eldercreek
Sacramento, CA 95824

Hillcrest Oriental Food Center
426 University Avenue
San Diego, CA 92103
Tel. (714) 298-0747

Que Huong
9087 Bolsa Avenue (Bolsa Plaza)
Westminster, CA 92683

China Trading
271 Crown Street
New Haven, CT 06511

Vietnam House
242 Farmington Avenue
Hartford, CT 06105
Tel. (203) 524-0010

Asia Market
1241 East Colonial Drive
Orlando, FL 32803

Oriental Food
2111 Rogers Avenue
Fort Smith, KS 72901

Kim Thanh
3003 Florida Boulevard
Baton Rouge, LA 70803

Tien Nha Trang
1804 Baratario Blvd.
Marrero, LA 70072

Tan Duc (Sonico)
214-216 Grand Street
New York, NY 10013

Thuan Nguyen
82 Mulberry Street
New York, NY 10013

Viet Nam Market
2702 E. 15 Street
Tulsa, OK 74104

Thai Binh
8th Street
Philadelphia, PA 19147

Vietnam
Christian Street
Philadelphia, PA 19147

Hoa Binh
2800 Pravis Street
Houston, TX 77006

Vietnam Plaza
2200 Jefferson Street
Houston, TX 77006

Tan Viet Market
10332 Ferguson Road
Dallas, TX 75228
Tel. (214) 324-5160

Xuan Thu
P.O. Box 720065
Houston, TX

Viet Nam Food
610 South State Avenue
Salt Lake City, UT 84111

Mekong Center
3107 Wilson Boulevard
Arlington, VA 22201
Tel. (703) 527-2779

Vietnam Imports
922 West Broad Street, Rte. 7
Falls Church, VA 22046

Viet-My Corporation
1007 St. Stephen Road
Alexandria, VA 22304
Tel. (703) 370-2234

Index